# ENCOUNTERING
## GOD IN THE OLD TESTAMENT

# ENCOUNTERING
## GOD IN THE OLD TESTAMENT

*Jacqueline McMakin*
*and*
*Rhoda Nary*

## HarperSanFrancisco
*A Division of HarperCollinsPublishers*

*Encountering God in the Old Testament.* Copyright © 1993 by Jacqueline McMakin. All rights reserved. Printed in the United States of America. No part of this book may be used or reproduced in any manner whatsoever without written permission except in the case of brief quotations embodied in critical articles and reviews. For information address HarperCollins Publishers, 10 East 53rd Street, New York, NY 10022.

FIRST EDITION

*Library of Congress Cataloging-in-Publication Data*
McMakin, Jacqueline.
    [Doorways to Christian growth]
    The doorways series / Jacqueline McMakin and Rhoda Nary.—1st ed.
        p. cm.
    Originally published as a single volume in 1984, under the title:
Doorways to Christian growth.
    Includes bibliographical references.
    Contents: [1] Encountering God in the Old Testament—[2] Meeting Jesus in the New Testament—[3] Journeying with the spirit—[4] Discovering your gifts, vision, and call.
        ISBN 0–06–065377–9 (v. 1).—ISBN 0–06–065378–7 (v. 2).—ISBN 0–06–065379–5 (v. 3).—ISBN 0–06–065380–9 (v. 4).
        1. Christian life—1960-    2. God—Biblical teaching.    3. Jesus Christ—Person and offices.    I. Nary, Rhoda.    II. Title.
    [BV4501.2.M4358 1993]
    248.4—dc20                                                    92–53917
                                                                      CIP

93 94 95 96 97 ❖ RRD(H) 10 9 8 7 6 5 4 3 2 1

This edition is printed on acid-free paper that meets the American National Standards Institute Z39.18 Standard.

# CONTENTS

# INTRODUCTION

Swiss psychiatrist C. G. Jung was once asked if he believed in God.

"I don't need to believe, I know," was Jung's reply.[1]

Who among us wouldn't want that kind of clarity? Who among us wouldn't like to stand up and shout, I *know* God.

On some basic level, each of us—the fervent believer along with the most tentative of seekers—would like just once to toss doubt to the side and directly experience the divine. Wouldn't it be nice, we cry, if God would stop us dead in our tracks and exclaim, "I am God. I am the heart of compassion. And who are you?"

This book is about the question "Who is God?" and about the way the people of a small desert tribe answered it more than three thousand years ago.

Their answer took the form of stories about their relationship with God, stories that are rich with image and populated with colorful personalities.

The collection of those stories gathered together form what we know as the Hebrew Scriptures or the Old Testament or First Testament. They take many forms. There are poems and prayers, allegory and reflective prose, history and parable. Their diversity is part of their strength.

If relationship with God is a room, these Scriptures are a doorway. There are other doorways to be sure, but when we find ourselves blocked from entering the room, it is comforting to know that these sacred stories are a portal though which many have passed before.

The importance of stories is appreciated anew in our culture. Scholar Joseph Campbell, who spent his life studying the myths of world cultures, describes a myth as a story that provides insight into the mystery of who we are. We need these stories, he claimed, because they provide us with "the experience of being alive." They are "bits of information from ancient times," he said, "which have to do with the themes that have supported human life, built civilizations, and informed religions over the millennia." They provide insight into "deep inner problems, inner mysteries, inner thresholds of passage." "Without the guidance of myths in life," he said, "you have to work it out yourself."[2]

This book focuses on six images of God experienced by the Hebrew people and woven into their sacred stories. It enables us to explore and relate these discoveries to our own lives. God was to this ancient people and can be for us:

✤ Creator

✤ Caller

✤ Deliverer

✤ Covenant-Maker

✤ Suffering Servant

✤ A New Song

Other images for God abound. In *The Divine Feminine*, Virginia Mollenkott focuses on feminine biblical images of God such as nursing mother, midwife, mother eagle, and Dame Wisdom. These images recover aspects of God that are lost when only male images are used.[3]

Verna Dozier, in *The Dream of God*, lifts up other images of God from the Hebrew people: the free God who "will never crush

our freedom",[4] who is "both for us and over against us",[5] who cannot be "fully comprehended."[6]

The six images of God that we listed, when taken together,
offer both grounding and impetus as we seek to live sensitively in
changing times.

For example, it is one thing to see that in some mysterious
way God the *Creator* formed the universe in the beginning of
time. It is quite another to know God as Creator of me, a unique
person with my own particular conglomeration of traits and tal-
ents, and to see that I am invited by God, the *Caller*, to be a co-
creator, continuing the life-giving work already begun.

Surely, in a world of frightening instability, to be a contribu-
tor to "building the earth," as Teilhard de Chardin put it, involves
risk, moving out, leaving behind familiar ways. It is then comforting to know God as *Deliverer*, "a very present help in trouble"
(Ps. 46:1, RSV).

Is there anything tangible to hang on to in this changing
world? God seemed to know our need for that. We are invited into
a relationship with God, the *Covenant-Maker*. This covenantal relationship with God is marked by tangible signs. At first these
consisted of blood, stone tablets, and the shepherding figure of
Moses. Today we are still invited into a covenant with God and
others and are challenged to make the Covenant tangible through
support and service.

As we become more involved with others through support and
service, we come up against the reality of evil. Hebrew people wres-
tled with the mystery of God's goodness existing alongside evil and
sin. The picture of God as *Suffering Servant* evolved as a profound
concept whose meaning we will never wholly grasp. But surely if it
means anything, it is that God does not love us in a casual, fair-
weather sort of way. The love of Yahweh gives everything, to seek
the lost, mend the broken, go after and woo the faithless.

We complete this course with God as *New Song*, a personal and realistic note on which to end. When Hebrew people faced challenges, they were brought to deeper communion with God, whose presence was revealed in fresh ways. This they celebrated in song and poetry.

We are invited to look for fresh contact with God in our present circumstances and to express that in song. Sometimes our songs are happy, sometimes sad, bewildered, lonely. Like the Hebrew people, we bring to God our deepest feelings and experiences and once again know God as present, creative, calling, helping, and steadying in all kinds of spiritual weather.

# PREFACE TO
# THE DOORWAYS SERIES

Two of us were rambling along a trail on a sparkling spring day. One was discouraged, did not know where her life was going. The other felt content and grateful for time to see what was happening in the woods.

Suddenly we stopped. Across our path lay a branch, broken off and seemingly dead. But there right on that branch burst forth a blossom that beamed at us in greeting.

We looked at each other and smiled. In that flower, God had broken in on us with a message: life can burst forth unexpectedly and bless us with its presence.

This brief story came to mind as we were thinking about the purpose of the four books in the *Doorways* Series. They are for people with hope, energy, and commitment who want reinforcement. They also are for dispirited people who question the direction of their own lives and of society.

The books invite you to taste nourishing spiritual food discovered by people in one particular faith path—the Christian tradition. From the core of this tradition radiates an astounding truth: there is at the heart of the universe a cherishing presence that holds all creation in a loving embrace. To be nurtured by this love is to be infused by fresh life.

In a fast-moving, multifaceted society, people look for anchors to hold them steady. Mobility makes us long for a sense of belonging. Pressing personal and societal needs make us wonder where we fit and how we can contribute.

The *Doorways* Series was written in response to these yearnings. It helps us listen to our own truth and sink our roots in a solid tradition. It takes us on a journey of discovery. Its purpose is to help us grow in spiritual awareness, learn to build community where we are, and be more fully God's person at home, at work, and in the other places where we spend our time.

Underneath our yearnings are profound questions. Each book in the *Doorways* Series focuses on one question most of us ask at one time or another:

✤ Who is God?

✤ Who is Jesus?

✤ How can I nourish my spirit?

✤ What should I do with my life?

To address these questions, this series offers twenty-four dynamic stories, images, and concepts found in the Christian tradition. When you allow your body, mind, and spirit to engage with these treasures, you will be enlarged, enhanced, empowered.

Included in each book are activities for you, the reader, as well as for a group. Thus, each book can be used as a course. Designed originally by a community of Catholic and Protestant laypeople, the courses include wisdom and practices from each tradition that we have found powerful in our own lives. The courses build on each other, but each can be used on its own.

In their time with Jesus, the disciples had a training experience—living, learning, doing. They moved from being neophytes to well-trained healers and teachers. These courses are designed to replicate this experience of growth for us twentieth-century people, to equip us to live the committed life. Each of the *Doorways* courses presents a different challenge.

*Encountering God in the Old Testament* provides a way to explore the understandings of God realized by people in the Old Testament. This introductory course is suited to people with no prior experience of faith as well as to longtime churchgoers who are taking another look at the meaning of faith.

*Meeting Jesus in the New Testament* offers opportunities to learn about the Jesus of history and to make faith decisions today in response to the living presence of the Spirit. It is for those who want to be more than observers of the ministry of Jesus, who want to explore being companions in that work.

*Journeying with the Spirit* is for those who are committed to the way of Jesus and who would like to strengthen that commitment through experiencing classic resources for growth such as prayer, meditation, healing, and reconciliation.

*Discovering Your Gifts, Vision, and Call* is for people concerned with the pain and disharmony in the world and who want to help implement God's vision for the world. It offers a discernment process for discovering one's gifts and calling as well as ideas for forming communities to give communal expression to it.

These four courses are progressive in that they build on a deepening relationship with God and provide opportunities to:

✤ *explore* experiences of God;

✤ *decide* about one's relationship to God;

✤ *deepen* those decisions;

✤ *discern* life direction and purpose.

We offer these books to each of you as you seek to find your particular way of making the world a better place. If current environmental degradation teaches anything, it is that every person on Earth must become involved in preserving this precious creation. To build the kind of global resolve necessary will require commitment and stamina, which come from being firmly rooted in sources of spiritual power.

# HOW TO USE THIS BOOK
## AS A COURSE

This book is designed not only to be read but to be used as a course for individuals and groups. As an individual, you can gain much from "doing" this book in your own way and in your own timing. Adapt the Group Design exercises to yourself and try them out. Do the Individual Work. Perhaps you can find another person with whom to share the course or to discuss some of its aspects. If you are motivated to work alone with the content, honor that instinct and have confidence that your efforts will bear fruit.

Groups that can benefit from the material are existing Bible-study, life-sharing, or task groups who want to grow together, or groups especially convened for the particular training offered through these courses.

## ✚ How the Material Is Organized ✚

Each book includes an introduction, six sessions, and ideas for further reflection and next steps. Each of the six sessions includes:

✚ Session Text: basic content material on the topic;

✚ Group Design: practical ways for a group to work with the content in the session text;

✚ Individual Work: suggestions on how to apply the content to our own lives as individuals.

## ✤ Using the Material in Groups ✤

In order to get the most from the course, it is important to do three things:

**1. Read and Digest the Text.**   Before coming to the first meeting, read the introduction, How to Use This Book as a Course, and the Session 1 text in preparation. To prepare for the second session, read the text for Session 2, and so on through the six sessions of the book. It is best to devote most of your time between meetings to the Individual Work related to the preceding session before reading the new session. Leave the new session for the day or so before you meet.

**2. Participate in the Group Design.**   When people relax and participate in the group activities, much growth occurs. No design is perfect, and no design works equally well for all groups. Don't be bound by these design ideas, but do take time to understand their underlying purpose. If you can accomplish the same goals in other ways, great. You may want to modify the timing on the designs. We estimate that our timing works easily for groups of about twelve people. Smaller groups will have more time; larger groups may have to shorten or omit certain activities.

Each Group Design has several parts that we will look at in detail.

*Gathering Time:*  The purpose of this is to assemble the group and ready yourselves for the session. Since we have built in ways to share personal information throughout the design, this does not have to be accomplished fully in the gathering time. Ten minutes is usually sufficient. Divide the time equally among all of you and really listen to each person. Resist the temptation to allow more time for this section or to be undisciplined in its use.

*Sharing Groups:* These are groups of four that you form at the first session. The purpose of these is to share in a small setting what you did with the suggestions for Individual Work and to support one another as you take the course. These same groups meet at least once during each session. We find there are many benefits when the same group meets consistently. To get to know others in the larger group, there will be activities to do with them as well.

*Discussion of the Session Text:* We have included discussion of the text only occasionally because we felt it useful to give more time to other activities. However, if your group would like to discuss it each time, feel free to do so. Here's a sample discussion question: What learning from the text was most important for you?

*Lab Exercise:* The purpose of the lab exercise is to enable the group to experience one aspect of the topic and reflect on this experience. The activities in this section vary a great deal. Some are lighthearted, while others are more serious. Participants have found them all to be valuable.

*Closing:* This time is meant to give people an opportunity to reflect on the session and to have closure. Sometimes we offer a suggestion about how to do this; at other times we leave it to you. Some groups like to vary their closing exercises; others like the consistency of the same ending each time, such as a favorite song or a circle of prayer.

*Materials:* We suggest that you bring a Bible and a notebook for each session. When additional materials are needed, this is indicated in the design.

*Breaks:* According to your group's needs, schedule a five- to ten-minute break in the middle of each session. Our estimated timing does not include breaks, so adjust your timing accordingly. Tell people at the beginning of the session when the break will be.

**3. Do the Individual Work.** This work is designed to be done at home between sessions and is an important part of the course. It is a bridge between sessions and provides ways for you to integrate the material. Our participants find this one of the most worthwhile parts of the experience and urge us to underscore it.

The individual work usually involves fifteen to thirty minutes of quiet time per day for reading, reflection, and writing your thoughts in a journal, usually a loose-leaf notebook. At the end of each week it is useful to write a one-paragraph summary of what you did, your particular learnings and difficulties, and any questions. This summary can be shared with the group.

We suggest that you devote the quiet times during the first part of your week to the Individual Work and use the last few days before your group session to read the new chapter in preparation for the next session.

For the six weeks of the course, budget the time you need to do the Individual Work. It is integral to the course.

## ✤ What About Leadership? ✤

Don't rely on just one person to make your group thrive. Leadership is needed for two functions: *facilitation* and *organization*. Consider finding two people for each function. Choose these people on the basis of gifts and motivation. Who would really like to do what?

*Facilitation:* This can be done by the same person or pair each time or rotated so everyone in the group takes a turn. As the group facilitator you will:

> ✤ read the session text, Group Design, and Individual Work in advance;

✤ gather the necessary materials for the next session;

✤ convene the group at the start of the session;

✤ lead it through the Group Design, keeping to the time you agree on;

✤ close the meeting with a reminder of the time and place of the next session.

There are additional ways you as a facilitator can help the group. You might:

✤ do some background reading.

✤ add your creativity to the Group Design, tailoring it to the needs of the group.

✤ pray for the people in the group.

✤ give examples from your own life to begin sharing times. The way you do this modeling is important. If your example is long, other people's examples will be long. If you share from the heart, others are likely to do the same. By your example you give others freedom to be open. Our participants tell us that when they hear leaders share authentic pains and joys, they feel encouraged to face similar feelings in their own situations.

✤ be attentive to nonverbal communication in the group. As a leader, you can foster an atmosphere of caring, genuineness, and openness through a smile, a word of encouragement, a touch on the arm.

*Organization:* This, too, can be done by the same person or pair each time, or rotated. To help in this way you can:

✤ publicize the course by placing notices in newsletters, making personal phone calls to invite people to attend, and distributing flyers;

✤ be attentive during the session to people's reactions and lend encouragement to those who need it;

✤ call absent people between times to fill them in on what happened;

✤ see that refreshments are provided, if the group wishes them;

✤ pray for the individuals in the group.

We call the organization people *shepherds* since they look after and care for each person individually, leaving the facilitators free to care about group process and content. After facilitating courses with the assistance of shepherds, we would never be without them. They make a major difference in the quality and depth of a course. Shepherding is a wonderful gift that some people have and enjoy using.

## ✤ How to Gather a Group ✤

Suppose you would like to gather a group to take a *Doorways* course together. Find another person who will work with you and who has enthusiasm about doing the course. Consider whether to seek church sponsorship. To find people who would like to take the course and to prepare them to participate fully, you can do these things:

1. *Spread the word as widely as possible.*

Start with family, friends, neighbors, members of groups active in the church and community, and newcomers. Try to contact these people personally. Tell them the purposes of the course:

to provide spiritual nourishment, to build a caring and supportive group, and to discover which part of God's work we are called to foster. (To become clearer about the purpose for each course, read the introductory material in the beginning of the course.)

People respond to an invitation to join the course for a variety of reasons: some are looking for a sense of belonging; others want purpose or direction in their lives; others are hungry for spiritual nourishment. Find out what people are looking for and then describe how the course addresses that need.

2. *Be sure to go over procedural matters such as the dates, time, and place for the course.*

If possible, hold the course in a comfortably home-like atmosphere.

Explain that the course depends on the commitment of all the members to come regularly, to be on time, to do the Individual Work, and to let someone know if they will be absent so they can be brought up-to-date before the next session.

3. *Let people know that the method used will be experiential learning.*

This style depends on the participation of each person and not on the expertise of a leader. Participants learn by doing. You each proceed at your own pace and in your own way. Some people will have important insights during the group meetings; others may have them at home; others may see results from the course only after it has ended.

This style of learning contrasts with traditional ways of teaching in which someone in authority (a theologian, pastor, or teacher) offers content to a learner, whose main job is to assimilate and apply it. Some people may expect a traditional aproach and ask questions such as "Who's teaching the course? Who's the leader?" Sometimes we offer this explanation: The traditional approach is useful for imparting doctrine (the wisdom and teachings of the church throughout history). Experiential learning enables us to examine some of those doctrines and make them a living part of our lives. The facilitators of the course are learners with all the others who take it.

4.  *Pray together for the group.*

That can make the difference between gratitude and frustration in gathering a group. When you pray, you may be given inspiration about new people to contact or new ways to do it.

5.  *Determine the size and makeup of the group.*

The course works well with groups numbering from ten to twenty, people of all ages, clergy and laity, men and women.

# SESSION 1

# Creator

The opening chapters of the Bible contain some striking ideas about God and people. The very first description of God is that of Creator: "In the beginning God created . . ." It is as if the writer wanted to reaffirm faith in God as the origin of life despite the apparent hopelessness of the circumstances.

In this session we will consider how the Hebrew scriptures portray God's creative action and how we participate in it.

The first creation story (Gen. 1:1–2:4) was probably written during the Exile, that painful period when the Hebrew people had been conquered and sent to Babylon in defeat. The Hebrew people had thought of Yahweh as a God of victory, a bringer of grandeur, power, and unity to Israel. How tempting now to conclude that the apparent destruction of the blessed nation meant also that God was dead!

But no, the opening note is one of hope—God, *first of all, is Creator*. No matter how devastated my nation, thought the Hebrew poet, the creative energy of God still lives. It is dependable, able to bring forth beauty out of darkness.

Second, the opening lines in Genesis affirm that *everything created is of God and is good*. The author portrays God as creating the world in six days and resting on the seventh. During those six days, out of chaos God formed light and darkness, night and day, land and sea, sun and moon, plant life, all living creatures on land and in the sea and air, and finally, humankind. Four times in the passage, God is portrayed as looking at what had been created and finding it good. And at the end of the account, Yahweh declared that everything that had been created was "very good"—a tremendous affirmation of the goodness of all creation. And further, an implied but crucial corollary: no living creature is left out of this goodness.

In the crushing humility of political defeat, the Hebrew poet contemplates the awesome goodness of the created order, reveling, as does Thomas Berry today, in the universe as "a single gorgeous celebratory event."[1]

Third, the writer goes on to a daring assertion: *All people are created in the image of God*. The creative energy of God, the ability to bring form out of chaos, is given to human beings, who in turn are instructed to be fruitful. People are invited to be co-creators with God, to have a part in continuing the creation. That part is our power to love and to give birth—to birth babies, to create farms, quilts, tools, schools. Our hands produce things; our hearts reach out in love; our minds birth philosophies.

The second creation account (Gen. 2:4–25) describes God's creation of male and female, Adam and Eve. God gives to them a garden to cultivate, the company of each other, and the invitation to name the animals and birds. In the garden, God is portrayed as walking and talking with Adam and Eve.

This vividly illustrates a fourth perception about God held by the Hebrew people. Not only a cosmic force responsible for the immensity of creation, *God is also a personal reality concerned with the particularities of each person's existence*. After describing the idyllic garden existence of Adam and Eve, the second creation account proceeds to wrestle with questions of personal freedom, choice, and suffering. People are free to cooperate with God's creativity, to respond to God's love. Or they can open up chaotic and destructive possibilities out of harmony with the order envisioned by God.

As retired teacher and biblical scholar Verna Dozier writes:

> We have missed the meaning of what it is to be created in the image of God. It has nothing to do with looking

like God. It has to do with God's freedom. . . . That freedom is the image stamped on only one creature—the human being. That creature could choose to be as God wanted it to be, or it was free to choose another way.[2]

The misuse of our potential to join God as co-creator is, according to theologian Matthew Fox, a sin. To use our creative potential in any way that destroys or harms our planet and all the life on it is a violation of the divine invitation to fruitfulness.[3] Whenever we say "I can't," as in the expression, "I can't be creative," or "I can't change anything," or "I can't be mystical," we accept the fallacy that we are powerless. We act as if our imagination were dead, denying that we are made in the image of God.

If we want to cooperate with God's creativity, it is helpful to understand what creativity is and is not. It is not something you do only on weekends, writes Rollo May in *The Courage to Create*.[4] We are not "dealing with hobbies, do-it-yourself movements, Sunday painting, or other forms of filling up leisure time." No. Creativity means "bringing something new into being," May states.[5] Paintings, yes, but also "new forms, new symbols, new patterns on which a new society can be built."[6]

We are faced with a choice in this time when

one age is dying and the new age is not yet born. . . . Shall we, as we feel our foundations shaking, withdraw in anxiety and panic? . . . [or] Shall we consciously participate, on however small a scale, in the forming of the new society?"[7]

If we opt to use our imagination constructively, we will experience the many components of the creative process. May describes the creative breakthrough in terms of *gratification, joy,* and "participating in an *experience of elegance.*" This breakthrough also entails *rebellion* and *rage* against things as they are. It involves valuing the *nonrational* as well as the *rational*. *Anxiety* is a prime ingredient, as our previous ideas and relationships are shaken up.[8]

The creative act involves an encounter of the individual with the world, an encounter that involves *real engagement, absorption,* and *commitment*. Paradoxically, the precise moment of creative breakthrough often occurs in a period of *letting go, relaxation, solitude*, or *disengagement*, and sometimes in *opposition* to the conscious idea to which one is clinging.

Contrary to the generally held notion that unlimited freedom is essential to creativity, May contends that "creativity arises out of the tension between *spontaneity and limitations!*" Indeed, limitations can be a catalyst for creativity, as can *ambiguity*.

May concludes that this sometimes frightening array of ingredients requires courage in the creative person. The courage we need is not the absence of despair. "We shall often be faced with despair, as indeed every sensitive person has been during the last several decades . . . [courage] is, rather the capacity to move ahead *in spite of despair*."[9]

These are some of the experiences we will have as we attempt to live out our birthright to be co-creators with God. For the Hebrews, this presupposed being in faithful relationship with the Creator.

The creation stories in Genesis 1 and 2, although written in two periods of history by two different authors, were used to form a prologue to the history of the Hebrew people. The writers believed the Hebrew people to be selected by God to reveal the kind of relationship God desires with the whole created order. As Robert McAfee Brown points out, biblical writers were not trying to prove the existence of God. Rather, they were describing how God is revealed and what that revelation has to do with people. They were not talking about an idea of a "something somewhere" that might or might not exist. They were talking about the living Reality who had confronted them, changed their lives, and entered into relationship with them."[10]

God's existence is not proven but taken for granted, since the writers feel they know God and are known by God. Brown continues,

> Put another way, what we find in the Bible is not an accumulation of data about God, but a living God in living relationship with people. These people have not lifted themselves by their own bootstraps into the presence of God. They testify that God has taken the initiative and sought them out.[11]

Brown's words offer clues about how we can approach God through the Bible. If we keep these sacred stories at arm's length and use them for objective study only, we will come away simply with more knowledge about Hebrew encounters with God. But if we see the story of the Hebrew nation as the story of everyone, including us, and seek to enter into a living relationship with a living God, then we may find changes occurring in us as dramatic and as creative as any described in the Bible.

One woman experienced a time of chaos and extreme darkness when her marriage unexpectedly broke up, leaving her bewildered and anguished. She reached out to friends whose faith in God seemed to sustain them and gradually became aware of a loving relationship with God deepening within her. The Bible began to speak to her in new ways. Passages from Isaiah resonated with her experience of God's faithfulness and love. Eventually, life began to flow and with it a new creativity. She was able to address a challenging work situation with new approaches, improve complicated family relationships in creative ways, begin a major writing project, and offer ideas to support friends in need of help.

When we have a living relationship with the living God, even with a limited human capacity, we can still join God in continuing the creation. A young high schooler with severe learning handicaps made a Sunday worship service truly memorable. With warmth and enjoyment she took up the collection and then simply prayed, "Here is our money, God. Please do what you want with it." Later, she again prayed very directly, "Please be with the hostages, God."

Somehow her simplicity and directness cut through all our wandering thoughts and placed us in a deeper reality. She was a principal creator of that worship service in a way that more apparently talented people were not.

Practically, how can we become more aware of the relationship God wants with us? One way is to allow the life-giving images of God discovered by the Hebrew people to live in us. Daily, through the media, we are exposed to life-denying perspectives. Why not devote equal time to an alternative view?

Mark Gibbard, Cowley Father from England, introduced us to a way to do this called "Bible pondering." This is different from Bible study, through which we attempt an intellectual understanding of biblical content. Such study is important as a background for Bible pondering but is not a substitute for it.

Bible pondering involves a heart understanding. Choose a short passage, phrase, or word. Allow its implications to penetrate your life, thought, and feeling. Ponder, for example, "God said, 'Let there be light'; and there was light" (Gen. 1:3, RSV). You might bring before God a particular situation. Suppose you are having a hard time with John at work. Picture God's light surrounding the two of you. Ask a question such as, "God, in what ways do you want to illumine my relationship with John?" Perhaps a request will occur to you. "Help me to see John as cherished by you." A word of thanks might come forward: "For hope that I can see John as you do, thank you."

Designate at least fifteen minutes for this pondering. Choose an inviting and a convenient place—a walk outside, a comfortable chair at home, or a quiet place at work. Make this your "oasis time" of refreshment.

Bible pondering can be done both alone or in a group. In our first Group Design, we present an opportunity for you to try pondering together, using a paraphrase of the material in Genesis 1 and 2. That part of the session demonstrates the kind of reflection and writing each of us can experience regularly in our times of meditation.

## GROUP DESIGN

*Purpose:* To get acquainted, share our hopes for the course, discuss our past experience with Scripture, and meditate on and respond to God as creator.

*Materials:* Marking pens, 8½ x 11 paper.

## A. Gathering Time, Everyone (*ten minutes*)

Using about one minute, share anything you like about *your name*—first, last, married, maiden names. Here's an example:

> My name is Phillip Parker. I feel pretty good about both names. I like Phil because it's not too common, yet most people are familiar with it. Parker is all right, too. It's easy to spell and pronounce. Of course, as a kid, I took a

lot of ribbing as somebody who could not be trusted by the girls if I asked them to take a spin in the car.

## B. Sharing Groups, Small Groups
(*twenty minutes*)

1. *Move into groups of four:* Be with people you don't know if that is possible. This will be the group with whom you'll gather each time to share what you did with the individual work and to support one another as you take the course.

2. *Exchange names:* Jot one another's name and phone numbers in your notebook for ready reference.

3. *Briefly share hopes and expectations for the course:* Consider jotting down each person's hopes so you can hold these in prayer.

*Note on sharing:* Speak from your own experience and to the point at hand. Always feel free to refrain from sharing if you wish. Remind one another of this occasionally if appropriate.

## C. The Bible in Our Past, Same Small Groups
(*thirty minutes*)

1. Take about five minutes to reflect in silence on your past experiences with the Bible. Ask yourself:

✦ Was the Bible life-giving?

✦ A dusty book on a shelf?

✦ Something people used to judge your behavior?

2. As thoughts and memories occur, take five more minutes, using some marking pens, to depict on a piece of paper some of

your experiences. Use color, form, lines, simple drawings. This is not meant to be great art but simply a way to engage the right side of your brain—the part that is creative and intuitive. Throw caution to the wind and simply symbolize on paper some of your past experiences with the Bible—whatever they have been for you.

3. When everyone is ready, briefly discuss what you did and why. If there are four in your group, you should have about five minutes for each person.

## D. Meditation and Sharing—God as Creator, Large Group, Different Small Groups (*fifty minutes*)

1. *Meditation read by one person in a slow and relaxed fashion:* "The following meditation on creation is designed to introduce the group to meditation or Bible pondering. It is a paraphrase of Genesis 1 and 2 that summarizes the message in those chapters. It is written as if it were the voice of God speaking directly to you.

"Before beginning the meditation, get in a comfortable position, with paper and pencil in hand. (*Pause while people do this.*) Take a few minutes of silence to quiet down. (*Pause.*) Be still outwardly and inwardly; closing your eyes might help. (*Pause.*) Imagine God in the room with you. (*Pause.*) Listen not just for the words that are read but for what message there is for you from God. (*Pause.*)

"I will read the first paragraph of the meditation twice. When finished, I will say, 'Respond.' At that time I will pause and give you time to respond inwardly and to jot down your responses. When people have finished writing, I will read the second paragraph slowly, ending with 'Respond.' Then there will be a pause for reflection and writing. Don't worry if some people write a lot and others don't. The main thing is to listen, reflect, and respond honestly in your own way. Sometimes that response might be a blank. That is okay. Now I will begin." [Read slowly, pausing after each sentence, so that people can picture what you speak about.]

## ✤ Meditation on Creation ✤

"Creation has begun. In the beginning there is darkness everywhere. See the darkness. Everything is a wasteland. It has no form. But it is *mine*. I am a creator. I create out of chaos. I create out of nothingness. [Repeat.] Respond. (*Reader pause for several minutes, allowing time for reflection and writing.*)

"Let there be light. I separate day from night. The wasteland becomes fertile, full of green. There is water, fish, animals. Day by day I create. There is order here. I am an orderly God. I have a harmonious creation. And it is good. Respond. (*Reader pause as above.*)

"I have formed you—out of clay, out of earth. I have breathed my breath into you. Breathe now, deeply. Hear the sound of my breath in you. Just breathe. My breath is all around. It mingles with my creation. In my image I create you. Male and female I create you. Companionship is good. Respond. (*Reader pause as above.*)

"I bring the animals before you. You name them. You co-create with me. You name things, know things, are fruitful. Your love names and creates. You have responsibility in this good place. I give you these things . . . to care for. Respond. (*Reader pause as above.*)

"I settle you in a fertile land. I am fertile. I walk with you. I talk with you. I feed you. There is union with me if you wish it. Respond. (*Reader pause as above.*)

"Now let us end our meditation."

2. *Sharing instructions read by the one who read the meditation:* "If we wish, we can share some of our responses in small groups.

Move into new groups of three or four. Go around the circle, each sharing our response to the first paragraph. Then go around again and share the second, and so on. Remember, if you prefer not to share, that is fine. Just say 'pass.'"

## E. Closing, Large Group (*ten minutes*)

Choose a way to close that is appropriate for your group. Possibilities:

1. Evaluate this session. (In a few words, what was helpful? What was not helpful? Suggestions for change.)

2. Sing.

3. Pray (give thanks to God who creates us and invites us to join in that creation).

4. Discuss details of the next session if necessary (time, place, leadership responsibility).

## INDIVIDUAL WORK

*Purpose:* To establish a regular time to be alone with God and to meditate on the meaning of creation for us personally

We suggest that you arrange to have a quiet time regularly for fifteen minutes (or more). Don't be discouraged if it is difficult to find such time. It is hard for everybody, but do not give up too easily. See this as a gift to yourself, an oasis of quiet, peace, and creativity.

1. *Read:* Use your quiet time the first day for some Bible study. Read Chapters 1 and 2 of Genesis. Get the full sweep of these passages. Try to understand what they are saying about God as Creator, about God's design for the world and for you in it. You also might review the session text.

2. *Meditate:* During each quiet time after your initial study day, select a theme, word, or phrase in these passages that draws you, stirs you, or freshens creativity in you. Sit with it quietly, allowing its meaning to deepen within you.

3. *Write:* Jot down in your journal any insights that occur to you. Consider writing on these questions:

✙ In what ways do I personally cooperate with creation?

✙ In what ways do I thwart it?

4. *Pray:* Respond to God out of your ponderings. Also use a few minutes to hold the people in your sharing group before God. You might want to look at their names in your notebook and visualize them receiving some of the blessings of creation.

5. *Bring:* Bring to the next session an object that symbolizes your experiences of God as Creator this week.

6. *Summarize:* At the end of the week, write a paragraph summarizing what you did with this assignment. Be brief, honest, and to the point. This will help you consolidate your experience and learnings and prepare you for the next session.

# SESSION 2

# Caller

When young people are eighteen, they may vote, but many don't. They feel their vote does not count, and more disconcerting, they feel their lives do not matter.

Hebrew people had a different idea. They saw each of us as a key player in the divine plan. They believed we are all called into a relationship with God and asked to extend God's love and justice. This session looks at how this happened to Sarah, Abraham, and Moses and then focuses on how people experience call today.

Picture elderly Abraham and Sarah enjoying retirement life. One day Abraham announces that he has heard a special call from God:

> Go forth from the land of your kinsfolk . . .
> to a land that I will show you.
> I will make of you a great nation,
> and I will bless you:
> I will make your name great,
> so that you will be a blessing.
> I will bless those who bless you
> and curse those who curse you.
> All the communities of the earth
> shall find blessing in you.
> (Gen. 12:1–3, NAB)

Abraham and Sarah's vocation was to receive and extend God's blessing to all the communities of the Earth—an important vocation indeed! They were to do this by establishing a nation whose way of living could truly be described as "blessed" and which would be a blessing to all (Gen. 12:2–3).

The Bible does not detail the responses of this remarkable old couple. It simply records that Abraham and Sarah gathered up their household and possessions and set out for the new land of Canaan. Once there, they pitched a tent, built an altar to Yahweh, and worshiped. After some time, God made the promise to Abraham clearer:

> All the land that you see I will give to you and your descendants forever. I will make your descendants like the dust of the earth; if anyone could count the dust of the earth, your descendants too might be counted. (Gen. 13:15–16, NAB)

When Abraham asked God how he could have descendants, because he and Sarah were childless, God assured him that the heir would be "of your own blood." By the time Abraham was eighty-six, nothing had happened, so he and Sarah took matters into their own hands and arranged for Abraham to conceive a child with Sarah's maid, Hagar. Finally, when Abraham was ninety-nine, God again approached him and reiterated the promise. God assured Sarah that she would bear a son, which she did when Abraham was a hundred years old. Sarah's reaction to all this was deep amusement:

> God has given me cause to laugh; all those who hear of it will laugh with me. (Gen. 21:6, NAB)

And so the child was named Isaac, or "God has laughed."

This improbable story carries some important truths. Abraham has always been described by the Jewish people as "faithful." Why? Not because of his total trust in God: he kept questioning the promises of Yahweh. Not because of his moral rectitude: he had tried to palm off his wife as his sister in order to save his own neck. Not because of his superior understanding of God: he seemed to need things repeated a number of times. It was because of what he did, how he acted, how he obeyed God's command to leave one place and move to another. Most important, Abraham was willing to enter into a relationship with God—a living, working partnership.

Throughout the Bible, God is portrayed as choosing to enter into a personal relationship with individuals and nations (at first the Jewish nation, later all nations), and calling them to special work.

For Abraham and Sarah, this meant saying "yes" to God's unlikely plan, moving to a new place, and parenting a son and heir.

For Moses, it involved returning to his people and leading them out of oppression in Egypt. When Moses heard what God had in mind, he wanted no part of it. His resistances are spelled out in Exod. 3–4:17. Moses had five objections to God's call, but Yahweh was ready with five responses. Here they are, slightly paraphrased:

Moses: Who am I to go to Pharaoh and bring my people out of Egypt?

God: I will be with you . . . and as a sign of this offer, worship on the mountain. (The promise of presence)

Moses: What shall I say to my own people when I go to them?

God: Tell them who I am, that I have seen their oppression and want to deliver them. (The promise of mission)

Moses: People won't believe me or listen to me. They won't believe you called me.

God: I will give you signs along the way that will provide meaning and reassurance. (The promise of support)

Moses: I'm not a public speaker—I can't think on my feet.

God: Go! I'll be with you and teach you what to say. (The promise of guidance)

Moses: Can't you send someone else?

God: All right. Here's Aaron. Take him. I'll instruct you in what to do; he can speak for you as your mouthpiece. (The promise of companionship)

The stories about Sarah, Abraham, and Moses have much to say about God and us. God is seen not simply as one who creates the world, winds it up like a watch, and lets it go on running by itself, but as one who chooses continually to be in a loving, creative relationship with us, one who calls us to special work.

In the Bible, naming has great significance. Often a relationship with God is sealed with a special name. God is seen not only as loving humankind in general but also as wanting a special relationship with individuals. Isaiah portrays God as saying:

I have called you by your name, you are mine. Should you pass through the sea, I will be with you. . . . Do not be afraid, for I am with you. (Isa. 43:2–5, JB)

When we are discouraged, two thoughts may occur: "I'm worthless. I don't fit anywhere." The promises to Sarah and Abraham strike basic chords in all of us: the desire to have our lives count for something, and to have a place, a home, our spot in the universe.

Both stories illustrate some important points about our response to God. The example of Abraham and Sarah assures us that no one is too old or too barren to become fruitful when touched by God. Moses shows us that past failure (he had killed an Egyptian in a fit of anger) does not disqualify us for present or future usefulness. Even inner resistance can be overcome if one listens for the guidance of God in specifics. What seems to be required is not great talent, intelligence, or attractiveness, but a willingness to say "yes" to God's invitation to collaboration and companionship.

People today hear and respond to God's call in different ways. Sometimes God's call comes directly, definitively: "Ever since I was seven, I knew I was to be a doctor." But for many, the process is gradual, beginning with a "whisper," as one person described it, rather than a definite call. Dag Hammarskjöld described this beautifully when he wrote:

> I don't know Who—or what—put the question, I don't know when it was put. I don't even remember answering. But at some moment I did answer Yes to Someone— or Something—and from that hour I was certain that existence is meaningful and that, therefore, my life, in self-surrender had a goal.[1]

Moses' experience gives us further clues as to how this works out in real life. For some people, hearing and responding to the call of God comes when they are absolutely alone. It was so with Moses when he was tending his sheep at the mountain of Horeb. He reported seeing a burning bush that was not consumed by flame. A voice called from the center of the bush,

> "Moses! Moses!" he said "Here I am," he answered. "Come no nearer. . . . Take off your shoes, for the place on which you stand is holy ground." (Exod. 3:5, JB)

Afraid to look, Moses covered his face. He was told that God knew of the oppression of the Hebrew people in Egypt and was sending Moses to bring them out of that land.

A moment of disclosure such as this is not as rare today as one might suppose. A recent Gallup poll found that many people have comparable experiences of God's presence. This is verified in our work with groups. We encourage people to look back over their lives and remember times that seemed to occur on "holy ground" —moments when an awareness of God was particularly keen, or when a burning issue within was somehow felt to be understood and blessed by God and experienced as a God-given task or mission. People in the groups frequently recall such times.

The first awareness of God's call may occur in a moment of inspiration. Sometimes the initial experience comes as a surprise. Seemingly, we have nothing to do with it. We feel visited or approached by God in ways we did not expect or earn. But as we seek greater clarity, we find that our own effort and decision come into play.

It is not easy to create that place of silence and solitude where we can have further dialogue with God. Author Dolores Leckey recalls how, as a busy young mother of four youngsters, she began to establish time alone with God in silence:

> A household full of small children, telephones, community and church responsibilities does not readily lend itself to silence. Yet my journey into books, my discussions with spiritual friends, my innermost instincts were all pointing to the need to be in touch with the experience of silence—quiet prayer. Hadn't God spoken to Elijah in a close-to-silent whisper? How would I learn to listen? I looked at the shape of a typical day and noticed some space. There was *nap time*, usually grasped at as an opportunity to accomplish tasks I couldn't get to when the children were awake. Shift, reverse. Instead of stuffing the space of nap time with various good deeds, I

stopped. I did nothing . . . or so it seemed. No radio, no
telephone, just silence. . . . I entered this mid-day Sab-
bath, sometimes with Scripture, sometimes with other
writings; often with restlessness and anxiety; sometimes
with eager anticipation and frequently with fatigue.
My time alone often ended in sleep, just like the children. "I give sleep to my beloved," sings the psalmist.
One thing became clearer and clearer. The less articulate the experience, the greater certitude I had of its
importance.[2]

In his silence, Moses brought complaints and objections to
God. In our groups, we encourage people to think about a call
they may feel or an area in which they would like to have a sense
of calling. Next, they are invited to address to God their resistances, reservations, or problems with that call and then to imagine the kind of reply a loving God might make to each of their
difficulties. It is surprising what breakthroughs can happen when
such a dialogue develops.

But before people can get started on such a dialogue, they
need to deal with their initial questions.

✛ What does a call feel like?

✛ How do I know if I am really called by God, or if it is a
figment of my imagination?

✛ What about the things I'm already doing—my job, my
marriage, my family? What if I first entered into them
without a consciousness of God's call? Can they become
a call?

✛ Does being called by God always mean leaving what
you're doing for something else?

✤ What if God calls me to do something I can't do or don't want to do? It's a scary idea. Is God going to require a sacrifice I'm too small to make?

✤ Can I have more than one call? Or does my call change as my life develops?

✤ Is God's call a general one, such as loving God and neighbor, or does it involve a particular work for me?

✤ Do I have to be at a certain level of spiritual development to hear God's call?

These are some of the questions that come up when we introduce the idea that God calls each one personally. Of course, a clear answer does not come for each of these questions at once. Clarity of call is an evolving thing and takes much time. Certainty or conviction about call seems to come and go. In Morris West's *The Clowns of God,* the former pope Jean Marie Barette experienced a call from God that was crystal clear, but listen to how he felt as he tried to live it out each day:

> Sometimes I am in a darkness so deep, so threatening, that it seems I have been stripped of all human form and damned to an eternal solitude. At other times I am bathed in a luminous calm, totally at peace, yet harmoniously active, like an instrument in the hands of a great master. . . . I cannot read the score; I have no urge to interpret it, only a serene confidence that the dream of the composer is realized in me at every moment . . . the problem is . . . that the terror and the calm both take me unaware. They go as suddenly as they come, and they leave my days as full of holes as a Swiss cheese.[3]

We need to be cautioned against forming too rigid an idea of call. If we learn anything from the biblical record, it is that call is experienced in countless ways. But several common threads run through these experiences. It does seem that those who feel called by God have at one time or another said *"yes" in as definite and wholehearted a way as possible*, however much they may have doubted later. Also these people continually position themselves to *listen to God*. They make space for time alone with God regularly and for longer periods of retreat. They *attune themselves to how God is working today* through contemporary reading, taking account of historical trends, participating in growth events, and talking with people who have a sense of call.

For some, call is quite general. Said one of our participants,

> I do not feel I am called to a specific task. I believe my call is simply to find and follow God.

For others, it becomes more specific. "I have loved being a life-insurance salesperson," declared Nedra Schilling in Harrisburg, Pennsylvania. "And I have felt it was a true calling."

Some have a lifelong call. "All my life the call to public service has inspired me," says a federal civil servant about his thirty-three-year career as a manager for the Agency of International Development. "I was lucky to find a place where I could combine my management training with my commitment to humanitarian assistance."

For others, call relates to a particular period in life. Mari Carmen Mariscal, a Mexican mother of four, is one of these. Attending a Chicago conference of La Leche League, the international movement that fosters breast-feeding, she agreed to be trained as a leader. In May 1972 an eager group of twelve mothers learned breast-feeding from Mari Carmen. "I felt called to do this even before I understood the word, 'call,'" she said recently.

It felt so right. I wanted to end hunger, to help families have better relationships, to see women empowered with greater self-confidence. This was a practical way to combine all three. It was something I could do while still busy raising children. Our movement spread in Mexico as it was growing in other countries. By attending and giving workshops in other countries, I gained a chain of friends all over the world—women of different languages, cultures, and economic means.

On November 20, 1991, at the Third National Symposium on Lactation in Mexico City, forty-nine Mexican hospitals were declared to be "baby friendly" since ceasing distribution of free formula and teaching the ten steps for successful breast-feeding. This declaration was announced in agreement with UNICEF, the Ministry of Health of Mexico, and the formula companies.

"After La Leche League being the lone voice for nineteen years," exulted Mari Carmen, "this was a religious experience. Thousands of doctors, nurses, and mothers are trained each year now in Mexico." All starting from one young woman who followed her heart and agreed to be trained.

Call can come at any age. As a youngster in school, Anne Keith remembers an English teacher who liked her writing. Yet it was only after her two children left home that she recognized the need to "go back to the embryonic writing that I had done in childhood and to plunge into the glory of words once more." She wrote a few poems in secret, then showed them to a friend, who was enthusiastic about them. Later, in her early seventies, Anne participated in a seminar for finding vocational direction. There she read her poetry to the participants, who encouraged her to do more readings and to publish her work. Anne sees her poetry as

a way of communicating the struggles and triumphs of experience as I try to accept the whole of life. Also I

am coming to realize that my age is a resource, not only
as a storehouse of remembered experiences and emo-
tions, but also as an ongoing pilgrimage through the
vicissitudes and graces of aging. Because I am further
along this road than most, I have something to say to
others.[4]

God's call may not be to develop a new work. One man, re-
flecting on call, said, "It wasn't that I felt called to do something
different after I dealt with Moses. Rather, I felt called to do what
I was already doing but in a different way."

As for waiting to achieve a feeling of adequacy or spiritual
maturity, remember that doubting Abraham, barren Sarah, and
resistant Moses were not perfect. They had limitations and handicaps like the rest of us. But they were willing to act in new ways.
So we invite you to open yourself to the idea of call and to the reality that you have unique experiences and capacities that only
you can offer.

## GROUP DESIGN

*Purpose:* To learn more about one another, reflect on a time of
closeness with God, and discuss our feelings and thoughts about
being called by God.

## A. Gathering Time, Large Group (*fifteen minutes*)

This is a way to connect with one another on the basis of
points of origin. Using about one minute for each person, share
your name and hometown. Then tell one good thing and one bad
thing about your hometown. For example:

My name is Ben Davis, and my hometown is Washington, D.C. A good thing about it is the stimulation of

living in the nation's capital. A bad thing about it is that many people are here for only a short time, so friends move away and leave us behind.

## B. Sharing Groups (*twenty minutes*)

Sharing what you did with the Individual Work reinforces your learnings and enhances your perspective through exposure to other people's experience.

1. Each in turn share what you did with the Individual Work. Tell one insight that occurred, a feeling you had, and a difficulty. Also report how it was to hold your group members and their hopes in prayer. Remember to keep your sharing brief and pertinent to what happened this week as you did the work.

2. After each person has had a turn, use the rest of the time to respond to one another. Share your feelings and thoughts candidly. Only in that way can you assess where you are and proceed from there.

*Note:* This is a time to check in briefly with one another rather than to share fully. It is not necessary to share everything on your mind, only that which is most pertinent to what you did with the Individual Work.

## C. Check-in Time on the Reading, Everyone (*thirty-five minutes*)

See if everyone read the chapter. If necessary, summarize the main points as a review. Then discuss what the session text said and your reactions to it. You might use these questions:

✚ What do I think of the statement that each of us is called to companionship and collaboration with God?

✤ Where am I in my response? Do I believe God is calling me? Do I want to hear that call? Do I want to respond? What are my hopes and fears as I consider my response?

✤ Regarding the questions on pages 34–35 of the text, can I illustrate them through personal experience, either my own or that of someone I know?

## D. Meditation and Sharing on a Holy Moment, Large Group (*forty minutes*)

This is a way to open ourselves to God's presence and to consider its meaning for today.

1.   Get settled comfortably with paper and pen for a time of quiet meditation. Be together in a few minutes of relaxed silence.

2.   Someone read aloud, slowly, the story of Moses' encounter with God in the burning bush (Exod. 3:1–6).

3.   Silently recall a time of closeness with God, a time when you sensed God's presence. It might be long ago or recently; it could be vivid and easy to recall, or more dim and difficult to remember. Be silent now and remember. When something comes to mind, get back into that experience; relive it. As you do this, describe the experience in writing. Where were you? What were you doing? In what way was God real to you? What awareness came to you? What was your response?

*Note:* Some people will write very readily and at length. Others will write very little. Perhaps some will not be able to recall such a memory or have not had such an experience. This is all right. Simply rest in the silence, noticing the thoughts that come. The learning for today may be that you cannot recall such an experience.

4. After everyone has finished, divide into groups of two or three, preferably with people not in your sharing group. Share what you have written, either reading or telling about the experience. Again, be brief. Give each person a turn before you open your session to general response. Feel free to pass if you do not wish to share.

## E. Closing, Large Group (*ten minutes*)

Choose one or two of the following as appropriate for your group: evaluation of session, song, details of next session, prayer of thanks for those times God has been revealed to you and to others.

## INDIVIDUAL WORK

*Purpose:* To examine our sense of calling, our problems with it, and ways God might help us.

1. Read Exodus chapters 3 and 4:1–17. Examine the call of Moses, his various objections to it, and God's response to each of his problems.

2. Reflect on an area in which you might feel called or would like to hear a call from God.

3. Like Moses, be honest about your objections or resistances to this call. Write them down.

4. In response to each objection, try to imagine and record what God's response might be. Remember that you are dealing with a loving, compassionate God who wants to offer illumination and help, not an angry God who wants to belittle or discourage you.

5. To prepare for the next session, write a brief summary of your personal work with this assignment as mentioned in Session 1, Individual Work, item 6.

# SESSION 3

# Deliverer

Christmas Eve, Moscow, 1991: worshipers bow and cross themselves, candles flicker, church bells peal, marking the first Christmas in seventy-five years in a free and independent Russia.

"The Christmas holiday has come back to us," television commentator Svetlana Sorokina rejoices. She adds,

> During the tough times we are living through now, many have no one but God to lean on. Any word from the church in such times brings hope.[1]

Calling anything associated with God "utter vileness," Lenin, father of the Bolshevik revolution, and his Soviet heirs tried to stamp out faith.

Yet some people held on. Christmas Eve they were in church. Nina Fyodorovna, seventy-eight, told a reporter,

> I always believed quietly and silently in my soul. I always prayed to God in the hardest times, and God always helped me.[2]

In hard times, God helped! True for Nina Fyodorovna. And true for the Hebrew people as well. This session focuses on how they became convinced of that help and how people today experience it.

No story reminded the Hebrew people of God as deliverer more powerfully than the account of Moses leading them out of Egypt. And no story has been used more widely to convey the same truth to oppressed people throughout history.

In Egypt, the Hebrew people lived in slavery under the cruel hand of the Pharaoh. Moses emerged as their leader. Although a Hebrew, he had been raised among the Egyptians by the Pharaoh's daughter.

After some time in the wilderness, Moses returned to his own people with a message: Yahweh wants to free you from slavery and bring you to the land promised to Abraham and Sarah.

Standing before the Pharaoh, Moses voiced these words of Yahweh:

> Let my people go, that they may celebrate a feast to me in the desert. (Exod. 5:1, NAB)

Pharaoh refused:

> I know nothing of Yahweh, and I will not let Israel go. (Exod. 5:2, JB)

Instead, Pharaoh increased their work load so they would not have time to listen to Moses.

Dreadful calamities, commonly known as the ten plagues, fell upon Egypt. The severity and rapidity of these events caused Pharaoh to attribute them to the angry god of the Israelites. Summoning Moses and Aaron in the middle of the night, he told them to be off quickly.

The Hebrews concluded that Moses was indeed a messenger from Yahweh and a worthy leader to follow. Leaving their homes for the desert, they celebrated a feast with unleavened bread to commemorate their safe deliverance.

Soon, however, they found themselves pursued by the Egyptians, who had changed their minds. This caused the Israelites to berate Moses for dragging them off to the wilderness:

> Far better for us to be the slaves of the Egyptians than to die in the desert. (Exod. 14:12, NAB)

Somehow Moses calmed their fears and convinced them that God would indeed again come to their rescue.

Then it happened! Just before the wind rose, Moses was able to lead the people safely across a shallow place in the Sea of Reeds. As the tide returned, it overwhelmed the Egyptian forces.

The wholly unexpected destruction of their pursuers filled the Israelites with wonder and thanks. The people "put their faith in Yahweh and in Moses" (Exod. 14:31, JB). With the prophetess Miriam leading, they exulted that Yahweh was their strength and song (Exod. 15:1–2).

They knew their deliverance to be due to no merit of their own. At the end of their resources, they had felt powerless in Egypt to do anything to obtain freedom. To them, their deliverance was miraculous: God had used the wind, the tide, and their pursuers' panic to save them.

Over and over, the Israelites remembered these events and saw them as proof that in hard times God cares and helps. They believed that in a special way God had selected them, a tiny, weak, often cowardly and ungrateful nation, as a vehicle for divine revelation. In dark nights of fear and oppression, God could indeed bring freedom and song.

What about today? What about us? Can we, do we, see and experience God as helper in hard times, as Deliverer?

There are people who, in the midst of political, psychological, or spiritual oppression, do experience God this way. They maintain an inner freedom and find an ability to sing a new song.

One thinks of Martin Luther King, Jr., composing his *Letter from a Birmingham Jail*. Or some of the returned hostages from the Middle East. Terry Anderson said that during his ordeal it was the Bible and a photo of his daughter Sulome that pulled him through. Benjamin Weir stated that three wires hanging from his cell reminded him of Michelangelo's Sistine Chapel painting of God reaching to Adam. "That became to me a representation of the sustaining purposeful hand of God," he recalled.[3]

Bruce Laingen, American hostage released from Iran, said that there were no hostages he knew of who failed to draw on religious strength during their ordeals. At times he admitted to feeling that "God must be sitting this one out." Yet in solitary confinement during nightly dialogues with God, Laingen repeated and was able to believe powerful faith statements in the psalms. A favorite was the great 118th psalm containing the same lines as the song of Miriam: "Yahweh is my strength and my song" (Ps. 118:14, JB).

Through the ages, the Exodus story has inspired oppressed people around the world. "Go Down, Moses" was the rallying song for black slaves; by it they signaled to one another their freedom of spirit and willingness to help one another use the underground railway.

Similarly, Bishop Desmond Tutu, leader in the struggle against apartheid in South Africa, says,

> You whites brought us the Bible; now we blacks are taking it seriously. We are involved with God to set us free from all that enslaves us and makes us less than what [God] intended us to be.[4]

The Exodus story points out that true freedom is not without risk and fright. You would think that if this were a story of deliverance, it would begin with danger and end with safety. Yet the reverse is true.

In Egypt the Israelites were not free. They were safe. A familiar way of life provided food each day and a roof over their heads. Their escape launched them into forty years of wilderness living, with no knowledge of how to find food and shelter and with no so-cial structure to which they could belong.

Why would God free them and then send them to the dangerous desolation of the wilderness? The answer seemed to be that deeper experiences of deliverance awaited them there—ones that could be experienced only away from familiar material and social support.

Hunger pangs fueled angry complaints against Moses. Instead of lashing back, Moses took these laments directly to Yahweh. Strangely, each evening flocks of quail appeared, enough for all to eat. And each morning, strange bread covered the ground. Enough quail and manna for each day but no more, necessitating daily dependence on God's help.

The people told Moses they were dying of thirst. Again they were delivered. God advised the hearty leader to strike the rock at Horeb and "water will flow from it for the people to drink" (Exod. 17:6, JB). Miraculously, that is exactly what happened. The place was then named Massah and Meribah, or "trial and contention," because that was where the people put God to the test by asking again, "Is Yahweh with us, or not?" (Exod. 17:7, JB).

In a third story, the Israelites were attacked by a tribe called the Amalekites. Battle leader for the Israelites was Joshua. Moses, taking his special staff, promised to go up on the heights (see Exod. 4:1–5 and 7:8–13). Arms raised in prayerful support, he encouraged the troops to keep fighting. As long as Moses kept his arms raised, the Israelites succeeded; but when he tired and let them fall, the advantage went to the enemy. Moses' companions, Aaron and Hur, gave the exhausted leader a stone on which to rest and held his arms up themselves. With this show of solidarity, the Israelites were victorious.

It was in events like these that the Israelites continued to experience Yahweh as deliverer. One psalmist wrote:

> Some wandered in desert wastes,
> finding no way to a city to dwell in;
> hungry and thirsty,
> their soul fainted within them
> Then in their trouble they cried to God . . . ,
> who delivered them from their distress,
> and led them by a straight way
> till they reached a city to dwell in.
> (Ps. 107:4–7)[5]

This psalm, prayed by Pastor John Robinson in 1620 with his little congregation, was the send-off for those embarking on the *Mayflower* to start life in the New World. It expressed his conviction that as these loved ones went from safety to the unknown dangers of a new existence, they would somehow, in unexpected ways, experience support, nourishment, and an inner freedom in the midst of struggle.

This must be something of what Rose Elizabeth Bird, former chief justice of California, experienced in her bouts with recurring cancer. In an address to a community forum on breast cancer, she described the devastation she felt when her disease flared up again and she realized her own physician had died of cancer. "As a direct result of these two circumstances, I went through a type of catharsis," she said. Learning all she could on the subject, she seriously pondered the possibility of having only a few years left to live:

> When you face the fact of your own mortality, you must also face the facts about what you have done with your life. In a peculiar way, death can teach you what life is all about. . . . I have learned much about myself, much about what I want out of life and much about how precious life and people are. It is our relationships with others, especially those whom we love, that give the

fullest meaning to life. I don't think I ever really knew that, emotionally or intellectually, until my second bout with cancer.[6]

In her personal desert, Rose Elizabeth Bird found in a new way the support of loved ones, the nourishment of hard knowledge, and a kind of inner liberation despite statistics and mortality rates on breast cancer. She concludes with encouragement:

> For those who are facing this disease and for those of you who may one day face it, let me say to you . . . have courage, face the facts, and you will find that when you have faced your fears and stood your ground there occurs a kind of liberation. . . .
> It is not a hopeless situation . . . it is an opportunity to find out about life. And isn't that really why each of us has been placed here?[7]

To relate to the Exodus story and discover its wisdom for us, we suggest using four steps for relational Bible study described by Karl Olsson in *Find Yourself in the Bible:*[8]

1. Make the story my story.

2. Identify with a character or element in the story.

3. Find good news in the story.

4. Name the story.

Here's how one group went through these steps.

1. *Make the story my story:* On newsprint, they placed the principal elements of the story such as Egypt, Moses, and so forth. Then the group together suggested words that describe each element. This is what resulted:

Egypt: Place of bondage, oppression

Red Sea: A boundary that needs to be crossed,
an obstacle to overcome

God: Opting for freedom,
practical—offered specific help

Moses: Persistent, tuned to a new vision,
not stuck in the old way

Israelites: Complaining, kicking and screaming,
moving, but not happily

Egyptians: Opponents of freedom,
plowing ahead despite destructive possibilities

Desert: Unknown, place of no support

Pharaoh: Fickle, looks out for own interests,
didn't care about people's suffering

2.  *Identify with a character or element in the story:* People identified with different elements. One person felt like a resistant Israelite because of her dislike of fund-raising, which was really
needed to develop her literacy program. The board, she said, had
Moses-type vision, expanded the scope of the program, and taught
her to raise needed funds. Another person admitted to feeling he
was his own Red Sea by allowing inner attitudes to become ob-
stacles to his creativity.

3.  *Find good news in the story:* Several people perceived that
in situations where they felt stuck, tangible help was available
even though they did not at first recognize it.

4.  *Name the story:* The best name suggested was "Don't Wail.
There's Quail!"

Close reading of these ancient deliverance stories reveals elements disturbing to the modern mind: the conviction that God sides with the "good guys"; that the good guys, with God's help, win; that violence is an acceptable means to achieve victory. Without much question, these beliefs were held by most Hebrews of that day. The biblical record, however, reveals development in their view of God and their part in God's vision. Beginning with the conviction that God chose them alone, they grew to realize that God's care extended to all nations and eventually saw themselves not only collectively but individually as instruments to make that known.

Additional questions arise. What is the nature of God's deliverance and to whom is it offered? Clearly, in ancient times Hebrews believed it included protection from bodily harm and was offered to those faithful to Yahweh. History provides us with ample evidence to the contrary. Bad things do happen to good people.

When Rabbi Harold S. Kushner learned that his three-year-old son Aaron would die in his early teens of a rare disease, he was forced to wrestle with these questions. His thinking can stimulate our own exploration of the nature of God's deliverance. In his book *When Bad Things Happen to Good People,* he concludes that although miracles do occur, the nature of God's deliverance does not in all cases include protection from physical harm. In his view, God does not suspend natural laws or intervene in human freedom to save from calamity one who has prayed. He concludes that life simply is not fair.

Kushner sees two ways that God delivers us from our suffering. First, God gives us "the strength and the perseverance to overcome it."[9] We open the door to such help when we move beyond the question "Why did this happen to me?" and ask, "Now that this has happened, what shall I do about it?" Kushner writes, "We, by our responses, give suffering either a positive or a negative meaning."[10] Then he adds,

> When people who were never particularly strong be-
> come strong in the face of adversity, . . . I have to ask
> myself where they got these qualities which they would
> freely admit they did not have before. My answer is that
> this is one of the ways in which God helps us when we
> suffer beyond the limits of our own strength.[11]

The second way we experience God's deliverance is through
the help of others. According to Kushner,

> God inspires people to help other people who have
> been hurt by life, and by helping them, they protect
> them from the danger of feeling alone, abandoned,
> or judged. . . .[12]

God summons forth friends and neighbors "to ease the burden and
fill the emptiness."

In addition to coming to us through the help of others or the
strengthening of our own resolve, there is a third way that God is
experienced as Deliverer that Kushner does not mention: unexpected, gratuitous awareness that the presence of goodness is at
our side. This just happens and seems to have nothing to do with
our readiness or other people's help.

There are times when we cannot recognize God as Deliverer.
We are left with pain, mystery, and questions for which there are
no ready answers. No matter how open we think we are, help from
others is not forthcoming and our inner resources are found wanting. It is then that we may feel God to be absent.

We are left with paradox. We experience God as absent, but we
also know that in the midst of suffering, when we feel most hopeless
and helpless, new life can and does break through. It is then that we
know God as Deliverer, a very present help in times of trouble.

# GROUP DESIGN

*Purpose:* To strengthen the sense of community among group members, to review some of the major biblical examples of God's delivering action, and to learn a method of relating biblical content to our lives.

*Materials:* Bibles, newsprint sheets, marking pens.

## A. Gathering Time, Large Group (*fifteen minutes*)

This is a way of strengthening the sense of community and caring. Standing in a circle, all share briefly what they left behind as they came to this session—for example, dirty dishes, some unmade phone calls, an important conversation. Then turn to the person on your right and give him or her a shoulder or back rub; you will be forming a connecting chain to do this. After a couple of minutes, turn around and rub the back of the person who just did yours. Then face inward and begin with informal prayer for the session.

## B. Sharing Groups (*twenty minutes*)

Each one share briefly the work you did with the Individual Work after Session 2 and how the prayer for one another went. Remember the basic suggestions for effective sharing: Make it brief, personal, to the point. If you prefer not to share, say that simply. No excuses or justifications are necessary. Be honest, and describe what happened this week with the assignment. Give everyone a chance to speak before offering responses or encouragement.

## C. Check-in Time on the Reading, Large Group (*fifteen minutes*)

If necessary, summarize the main biblical and contemporary stories mentioned in the reading, and the major points they are meant to illustrate.

## D. Relational Bible Study on Deliverance, Small Group, then Large Group (*sixty minutes*)

If you have not already done so, briefly review the instructions for relational Bible study in the text. Now divide into three groups, different from your regular sharing groups. Each group will do a relational Bible study on a different Scripture, choosing from these three: Exod. 16:1–21 (the story of the manna and the quail); Exod. 17:1–7 (the water from the rock); Exod. 17:8–13 (the battle against the Amalekites).

1. Each group move into different parts of the room, or if possible, different rooms, for privacy. One person in each group read the passage aloud.

2. List the principal characters or elements in the story, with descriptive words beside them.

3. Each one share the element or character with which he or she identifies and why.

4. Share what seems to be good news in this story for you.

5. Brainstorm on names for the story, and select one or two favorites.

6. Work out a way to present the story, the good news, and the name to the whole group. Consider doing a skit, a drawing, or using some other way to get the story across.

*Pointers:* Use about twenty minutes for the above. You will be working quickly. Go with first impressions. The mood can be light and fun even though you are dealing with profound material.

When all the groups are finished, present your stories to one another. As time permits, allow a few moments for discussion of the content or the method.

## E. Closing, Large Group (*ten minutes*)

Choose one or two of the following suggestions as appropriate for your group: evaluation of session, song, details of next session, prayer of thanks for times when God's deliverance has been real for you.

## INDIVIDUAL WORK

*Purpose:* To look at areas in our lives where we need God's deliverance.

1. We suggest the terms *Egypt* and *desert* be used to mean the following: Egypt—areas of bondage, oppression, or satisfaction with the status quo; dependence on things that prevent new growth (in self-understanding, social responsibility, etc.). Desert— where God can confront or test me and be revealed in a new way. During the week, meditate and journal on how these images apply to your own life. Feel free to let them carry you where they will. The following questions might be useful:

✤ What is an Egypt for you?

✤ What is a desert for you?

✤ Do you have motivation to leave Egypt? What is it?

✤ Do you need help to leave Egypt? What kind?

✤ What is happening to you in the desert? How do you react?

✤ What do you think God is trying to do?

2.  *To be ready for the next session:* Write a brief summary of your personal work with this assignment.

*Note:* These images strike people in many different ways. For some, they explain a great deal of what is happening to them. For others, they may not seem relevant at this time. But our experience is that it is helpful for all group members to try the exercises. Experiential learning of this kind has great staying power. If you go through the work now, it will be yours to draw on when it may be more pertinent to your life situation.

# SESSION 4

# Covenant-Maker

Powerful discoveries about God shaped the development of our spiritual foremothers and forefathers. The Creator brought form from chaos. The Caller invited each one to companionship and collaboration in continuing the creation. What was needed was a definite "yes" on their part, although frequently they gave a "no" or an evasion. When they did follow Yahweh, they had no guarantee against trouble. Yet even in difficult times food, drink, and guidance were provided by the One Who Delivers.

Leaving the familiar situation in Egypt for the unknown terrors of the desert, the Hebrew people finally arrived at the mountain where Moses had originally heard God's call. There, they heard an astounding invitation—to live in covenant relationship with Yahweh forever! This session examines the meaning of God as Covenant-Maker to the Hebrew people and to us.

When two people promise to share their lives together, supporting each other in sickness and health, they follow a ritual to celebrate. Rings are exchanged—tangible signs of something inexpressible. People witness and support the couple and pledge to be "their people." Community support is vital to the growth of love.

This is a form of covenant—probably the most familiar form we know. The words from the Latin mean "to agree." When lived fully, the agreement to love each other through thick and thin becomes a strong container in which to grow, to struggle, to learn the specifics of making this a reality each day.

"I will be your God and you shall be my people" is the description of covenant used all through Scripture. The understanding of what that meant to the Hebrew people and what it can mean today for us as individuals and as a community of inter-connected beings has steadily grown through the years.

In the early days of their recorded history, the Hebrew people conceived of the Covenant made only with them. From Mt. Sinai, Moses received this message from Yahweh for the people:

> You have seen for yourselves how I treated the Egyptians and how I bore you up on eagle wings and brought you here to myself. Therefore, if you hearken to my voice and keep my covenant, you shall be my special posses-sion, dearer to me than all other people, though all the earth is mine. (Exod. 19:4–6, NAB)

Yahweh's part in the Covenant was assumed. The nation's re-sponsibilities were spelled out in two ways: the familiar Ten Com-mandments (or Ethical Decalogue) in Exodus 20; the ceremonial version in Exodus 34.

Five religious responsibilities (loyalty to God alone, intoler-ance of idolatry, abstention from profanity, public worship, re-spect for parents) and five social obligations (protection of human life, of marriage, of property, of reputation, and restriction upon greed) provided the basis for forming the desert clans into a con-federation under God. These commandments were summarized in words, inscribed in stone, and then housed in an ornamental box called the Ark, which was carried with them as the people moved, and which occupied an honored place in the encampments. Yah-weh was thought to reside in the Ark but was not confined to it.

The desert Covenant between God and the Israelite confed-eration was sealed in a public ceremony involving sacrifice. Blood was sprinkled on the altar and the people to signify solemn bond-ing. Then a sacrifical meal was eaten.

As the tribes became more settled, the ramifications of the Covenant were spelled out in greater and greater detail. There

was danger that the original love pact would be buried under the
weight of rules and regulations.

It was against this type of development that the prophets
spoke out in later years. As the Kingdom of Judah crumbled, Jeremiah called his people back to the inward dimension of the
Covenant through these words of Yahweh:

> Deep within them I will plant my Law, writing it on
> their hearts. Then I will be their God and they shall
> be my people. (Jer. 31:33, JB)

And it was Jeremiah who concluded that the Covenant was
not with any one nation, but with all individuals who kept alive
in their hearts the fire of God's love.

The prophet Isaiah offered a poignant metaphor for Yahwah's
yearning love:

> Can a woman forget her sucking child,
> 　　that she should have no compassion on the
> 　　　　fruit of her womb?
> 　　Even these may forget,
> 　　　　yet I will not forget you.
> Behold, I have graven you on the palms of my hands.
> 　　　　(Isa. 49:15–16)[1]

References to the Covenant abound in the prophets and
psalms. New Testament writers conceived of Christ as an embod-
iment of God's covenant love for us and the Eucharist as a mystical interchange of covenant love.

Why all this emphasis on covenant? What meaning has it for
the Hebrew people and for us today? Though the wording and understanding of covenant changed and developed in the Bible, one
meaning remains constant: God's yearning love is expressed in
visible, tangible ways—ways we can see, touch, and feel. The

terms of the loving relationship God wants with us are clear, written down, and restated throughout the Bible in order to open us to the power that covenant can have in our lives.

When one glimpses the meaning and impact of God's covenant love for us, it is as significant and as life changing as when lover reaches to beloved with a proposal for lifelong commitment.

The biblical signs, understandings, and rituals are attempts to express the inexpressible. Our God is not a distant deity waiting to be discovered and worshiped. Yahweh reaches to humankind, cares deeply, goes after the lost, is faithful in the face of unfaithful response.

How may we respond to the repeated invitation to live in covenant love with God? The sacramental life of the church is one way. Through sacraments like baptism and Holy Communion, we are invited to say "yes" to a committed visible relationship with God. Participation in the sacraments, however, can become rote. That is why efforts to renew faith are important.

For many of us the true impact of God's covenant love does not come alive until we approach it afresh. We encourage people in our groups to address these questions:

✤ Can you consider the possibility of a covenant relationship with God at this time?

✤ Can you write a statement expressing such a covenant with God? (Include what you wish this relationship to be, what you will do to bring it about, as well as your understanding of God's part)

This is challenging. Not only does it offer you an opportunity to respond to God explicitly, it asks you to ponder concrete ways to live out your response daily.

When presented with this challenge, people have all sorts of reactions. Some are delighted and feel privileged to articulate their response tangibly. One of these people is Ruth Powell, the widowed mother of a friend of ours. In a beautiful book of quotations and photos entitled *The Widow*, her daughter Mary Clare portrayed Ruth's life in the period of adjustment after the death of her husband. Though she never used the term *covenant*, Ruth did indeed determine a way of living in covenant love for a whole year. This is how she did it, told in her own words:

> Very quickly, I drew a circle. In the center I wrote R and G—that stood for Ruth and God, meaning that I wasn't in this alone. Then I made pieces of a pie. This was what I wanted my life to be about at this present time.
>
> My physical life—food, clothing, and shelter. Food— I wanted to learn a few new things to cook. Things that were simple and healthful. Clothing—"Well, Ruth, you need to spruce up a little bit," I said, so I put a little emphasis on appearance and so on. Shelter— I knew that my house was to be part of a rehabilitation program any time now, and I would have to spend some of my efforts on that.
>
> A small slice was a little project that I was going to think up—doing something for somebody else. My little mission. I did think of a volunteer activity that I could offer at the North End School. So I initiated that, which I felt very good about.
>
> The next piece was the art of socializing—I put "Fun and Games" in parentheses. I had needs there. I knew I needed more fun. I needed some friends. I needed some social activities.

The last piece was the spiritual side of my life. I listed all the things I did that related to spirituality—worship on Sunday morning, the support group, the disciplines of the church, journaling, prayer, meditating on scriptures.

I shared my pie with my support group, and it was my work for the whole year. It was really nice because it was something very concrete you could look at and keep in mind. It was nice the way I had what was important drawn big—it helped keep me on the track.[2]

Unlike Ruth Powell, some people resist writing things down and asking others to help them live out their part of the Covenant. For some, covenant can seem heavy. When that feeling comes, it is helpful to try to think of covenant in down-to-earth, everyday terms. A teenager, Rachel, keen on becoming a cheerleader, tried out for the team. To her delight, she made it. As the year went on, her joy ripened into deep commitment and real appreciation for the opportunity. Good things happened. For the first time, she really belonged in the school. She had an identity with a group that had a purpose and was geared for action and disciplined for growth. She loved the challenge. She grew, reached out, shared her gift with others, sparked school spirit. The agreement was clear: "Come to every practice. Work hard. If you don't want the commitment, there are many who would be glad to replace you." In this arrangement, she throve!

Covenant with God is like that—a challenge, yes. A terror, no. God loves us profoundly and wants the very best for us. Responding in concrete terms does not open the door for God to do something terrible or beyond us, but to do something wonderful with us. Surely challenges will come our way, but then if Sarah and Abraham are to be believed, it is not great accomplishment that God looks for but simple faithfulness.

Throughout history, people have formed intentional communities to rethink and help one another live the Covenant in their particular time and place. Ignatius of Loyola, Francis of Assisi, and Teresa of Avila led companions into organizing the Jesuit, Franciscan, and Carmelite orders. In English villages, people inspired by John and Charles Wesley formed small groups called classes for learning the way of committed living.

Several women and men in our church formed what we call a "Covenant Life Group." Recognizing how far many of us were from family, two women gathered all "who want to explore forming a group to give each other personal support and to help each other grow." Haltingly, we explored how to proceed. Eight years later we are a community.

When we meet, we share something of how our lives have been since last being together, and we always close with a circle of prayer. We may also study a book, share some poetry, express ourselves through paint or clay, walk in the woods, or ham it up by putting on an impromptu musical. What we offer one another is faithful caring. Never absent save for emergencies, we are there for each other. Like Rachel with her cheerleading, we have a deep sense of belonging to one another, and we are growing in unexpected and unprogrammed ways. Each time, we leave the group empowered to be more caring and compassionate in other settings.

A current and hopeful development of covenant living is the recently published Earth Covenant. Recognizing the Earth as a sacred part of God's creation, an international group of global thinkers forged the Covenant which is now distributed by twenty partner organizations. Signature and "citizen ratification" campaigns are being planned at local, national, and international levels. Signatures to the Earth Covenant were presented at the World Conference on the Environment in 1992.

This is a first step toward further action, crucial for reversing the ecological crisis. The following excerpts are taken from the Covenant:

> We, the peoples of the Earth, rejoice in the beauty and wonder of the lands, skies, waters, and life in all its diversity. Earth is our home. We share it with all other living beings. . . .
>
> Yet we are rendering the Earth uninhabitable for the human community and for many species of life. . . .
>
> As citizens of the world, we accept responsibility in our personal, occupational and community lives, to protect the integrity of the Earth. . . .
>
> In covenant with each other and on behalf of the whole Earth community, we commit ourselves to the following . . . actions:
>
> ✤ . . . we will work to prevent ecological degradation
>
> ✤ . . . we will work for more equitable access to the Earth's resources
>
> ✤ . . . we will use environmentally protective technologies
>
> ✤ . . . we will work for the enactment of laws that protect the environment[3]

All of us—individuals, groups, and the whole global community—are invited to respond to God's covenant love in specific terms. When we do, important things can happen within us and through us. As we promise and carry out specific actions to live the Covenant, we deepen our life in God. As we support one another in specific covenants, there is a collective impact for good. We become what Arnold Toynbee described in 1935: a creative minority "turning to the inner world of the psyche," able to summon the vision of a new way of life for our troubled civilization.

God renews the invitation to covenant love in countless ways. How will we respond?

# GROUP DESIGN

*Purpose:* To evaluate how the group is progressing thus far, to renew our vision of God who desires a covenant with us, and to examine the difference a covenant makes in our lives.

*Materials:* Newsprint, a marking pen.

## A. Gathering Time, Large Group (*ten minutes*)

As you think over your life this past week, share one thing that has been important—for example, a project at work, a concern about a family member, a book. Collect these in a prayer, offering them to God and asking for God's presence with you during this session.

## B. Sharing Groups (*twenty minutes*)

Share briefly what you did with the suggestions for Individual Work after Session 3 and what this meant to you. Give each person a chance to speak before responding or entering into general discussion.

## C. Taking Stock (*twenty minutes*)

Since we are halfway through this course, it is a good time to take stock of how things are going. Do this first in pairs and then in the large group.

1. *In pairs:* Choose a person who is not in your sharing group. Speak about what is helpful in the course experience, and what causes difficulty. Take about three minutes per person. Be frank. One recurring comment we get in our evaluations is how important it is to be able to express a range of thoughts and feelings about the course.

2. *In large group:* Toss into the circle at random the thoughts and feelings that seemed most important in your sharing in pairs. In this type of growth, candid sharing can be both helpful to those who express it and catalytic for the group. For example, someone might say, "We're following the plan of the course in a wooden fashion. We're not touching the deeper places in our lives. It seems superficial." This frankness could trigger some beneficial thinking in the group about how to do things differently. It is best to let several comments surface before responding.

*Note:* We are suggesting only fifteen minutes for this large-group sharing. It is not important to solve all problems at this time, but it *is* important to encourage an atmosphere of honest reflection on the content and process of the course and receptiveness to suggestions for improvement.

## D. Sharing a Significant Relationship
### (*twenty minutes*)

1. *In pairs:* In the same pairs as in C, tell briefly about a person with whom you have had or now have a significant relationship of caring and support. It may be a family member, teacher, friend, or work colleague. Give a few details about the person, the relationship, and why you feel good about it.

2. *In large group:* In spontaneous fashion, address yourselves to this question: What are the characteristics that make this person special to you? Consider writing these characteristics on

newsprint so all can see. Then think and talk a bit about a most astounding fact: God's love for us has these same characteristics! That is the kind of God with whom we are dealing. Help that important fact to sink in.

## E. Covenant Today, Large Group (*thirty minutes*)

In a free-flowing discussion, talk about the difference covenant makes in our lives today. You might like to share some examples from everyday life like the story of Rachel in the text. What has happened when you have entered into a covenant (agreement) with another or with God, having a definite understanding of how it can be carried out? Remember that in the time allowed you will not be able to finish this discussion. The really deep consideration of God's covenant love is a lifetime affair.

## F. Closing, Large Group (*ten minutes*)

Choose one or two of the following suggestions as appropriate for your group: evaluation of session, song, details of next session, prayer of thanks for God's covenant love in history and today.

## INDIVIDUAL WORK

*Purpose:* To examine and make our own response to God's covenant love.

A common response to covenant is "It's wonderful that God wants to make a covenant with us—but I'm not worthy to enter such a covenant."

The book of Ruth is a wonderful response to that perception. By the standards of the day, Ruth had several reasons to feel worthless. She was a woman in a man's world, a foreigner among a nationalistic people, a woman without a husband in a society that related woman's worth to marriage. This beautiful story shows how the love that God wants for us overcomes all barriers we erect. It depicts bonding (covenanting) between God and humankind, male and female, alien and native, daughter-in-law and mother-in-law. We see covenant described in intensely human and poetic terms. At one point Ruth herself expresses her covenant love with Naomi in the words resembling God's covenant promises to humankind. She says, "Your people shall be my people, and your God my God" (Ruth 1:16, NAB).

Read this short book as background for reflection on the following questions:

In what ways does Ruth's story illuminate your own openness or resistance to commitment with God and others?

How do you personally want to respond to the covenant love being extended to you by God? Do you wish to accept such a relationship? Try writing a statement expressing your covenant with God. Include not only what you wish that relationship to be but what you wish to do to bring it about. It may be helpful to complete the following statements:

✤ A great hope I have in living out my covenant with God is . . .

✤ A fear I have is . . .

✤ In order to be more faithful to my covenant with God, I need . . .

To prepare for the next session, write a brief summary of your personal work with this assignment.

# SESSION 5

# Suffering Servant

It is one thing to see God as Creator out of chaos, calling people to assist in completing creation, delivering them from the bonds that thwart new life, and covenanting with them to solidify a creative relationship. But what happens when all tangible evidence of creativity is missing, when things fall apart, when collapse rather than deliverance happens?

These questions burned in the mind of the writer known as Second Isaiah.[1] What kind of God would allow everything we hold dear to disintegrate?

A strange image occurred to this troubled prophet: God is like a Suffering Servant. Words flowed:

> The servant was oppressed, and was afflicted,
> yet did not say a word;
> like a lamb that is led to the slaughter,
> and like a ewe that before her shearers is dumb,
> the servant did not say a word.
> (Isa. 53:7)[2]

And then, a puzzling paradox:

> On the servant "lies a punishment that brings us peace";
> and through the servant's wounds, we are healed.
> (Isa. 53:5, JB)

What was Isaiah thinking about? To probe the mystery of the Suffering Servant, we review the events that tumbled through Isaiah's mind.

Isaiah's people had felt chosen by God for the special mission of revealing divine compassion to the world. God had delivered them out of Egypt, into the desert, and then to the promised land.

There they met with ups and downs. At times united under strong kings like David, they held the land intact. But in weaker periods, they became worn down, resorted to civil war, and finally were destroyed by hostile neighboring nations. Sometimes loyal to the sacred Covenant, at other times they took on the religious practices of their conquering neighbors.

Finally, Jerusalem, their beloved political and religious center, fell to Babylonian aggression, the nation was destroyed, and the people exiled to Babylon. Crushed by these developments, the exiled psalmist wrote:

> Beside the streams of Babylon
> we sat and wept
> at the memory of Zion . . .
>
> How could we sing
> one of Yahweh's hymns
> in a pagan country?
> Jerusalem, if I forget you,
> may my right hand wither!
> (Ps. 137:1–5, JB)

Other people, however, saw light in the new situation. Jeremiah perceived the Exile to be a necessary discipline to purge people of misconceptions about Yahweh's true purpose for them. The blessed Covenant was made in the hearts of faithful people no matter where or in what situation they were.

Second Isaiah saw hope in the apparently desperate situation. Imagine trying to make sense of what had happened: the chosenness felt by the Hebrew people, the realization that God was the God of all nations, the tragic defeat of his people, their faithlessness to the Covenant. How could they hope? If God would not bring redemption through a strong political nation, or through a consistently faithful and moral people, how could Yahweh express love to the world?

It was then that the image of the Suffering Servant occurred to Second Isaiah. Profoundly moved, the inspired prophet wrote four Songs of the Suffering Servant, revealing the insights that came to him (see Isa. 42:1–9; 49:1–6; 50:4–11; 52:13–53:12).

The Servant embodies a radical new way of redemption, achieved not through political success or righteous purity, but through suffering, humiliation, and defeat. Bearing voluntarily the tragedy of life, the Servant is crushed. However, in the Servant's apparent defeat, humankind is healed. Silence is the Servant's most eloquent expression of caring. Rejected and misunderstood by people who concluded that suffering is caused by sin, the Servant refuses to protect himself. Although the Servant's suffering seems senseless, the Servant's behavior is redemptive to others.

Surprisingly, Isaiah saw God calling the exiles to embrace the way of the Suffering Servant to fulfill their historic vocation to be

a light to the nations,
that my salvation may reach to the ends of the earth.
(Isa 49:6, NAB)

For Second Isaiah, God was not only a strong deliverer but a struggling, suffering God who wept at violence and was crushed by cruelty.

The identity of the Suffering Servant is multifaceted. Surely, Isaiah portrayed God as the Servant. But certain passages lead one to conclude that he saw his own experience in that light as well. Some believe the Servant refers to the restored nation of Israel, or the remnant of faithful people, or a messiah. Christians have considered these passages descriptive of Jesus. Certainly Jesus read them and identified with them.

The Servant passages depict the suffering love of God in such a gripping way that it is possible through them to experience this love personally. Gifted by its power, people are fired to respond with such deep compassion for others that their lives resemble that of the Suffering Servant to whom they feel so indebted. Martin Luther King, Jr., Simone Weil, Mother Teresa of Calcutta, Archbishop Oscar Romero, and Elizabeth Fry come to mind. Less famous but no less noteworthy are the rare and wonderful people within our own families and circles who, though unknown and unsung, reflect this same compassionate courage.

Like all profound spiritual realities, the idea of the Suffering Servant is open to abuse. When misguided souls try to earn love through taking on suffering, a dangerous self-righteousness or false martyrdom can result.

By contrast, persons like the ones just mentioned are infused with a divine love they did not earn. Their responses to this surprising gift produce lives that are truly powerful. Their very presence inspires those around them. Their good work overflows from an inner experience of abundant love, of being so filled that it is natural to see oneself as a channel for that love.

This illustrates the paradoxical nature of the Suffering Servant. Alongside searing pictures of the Servant's suffering are glad announcements of the Servant's exaltation:

> See, my servant will prosper,
> he shall be lifted up, exalted, rise to great heights.
> (Isa. 52:13, JB)

This is the spirit made visible at the Hospice of Northern Virginia. More than 150 committed volunteers and staff enter deeply into the suffering of dying persons and their families. One gets the feeling that they enjoy their work. Something deep within is given creative expression. One person learns so much from her dying friend that she gains great joy from sharing it at the hospice. A weekend carpenter takes pleasure in using his skill to enhance a truly needed effort.

It is tempting to glamorize this type of giving and not see it for the mix it really is. Not only do staff and volunteers participate in the suffering of patients and families, they also take on the hardship involved in creating a new institution: missed deadlines, disagreements, disappointments, countless difficulties. The willingness to stay committed, to suffer through creating something new, to rise above rejection and lack of appreciation might cause many hospice workers to smile wryly at the biblical description of the Servant "harshly dealt with, he bore it humbly."

However, there are limits to how completely one person can share the suffering of another. You can empathize with another, alleviate some pain, be alongside, but never *fully* experience what is going on within that person. Only God can do that. *God* is the Suffering Servant. We are recipients of God's self-giving love and reflectors of it.

There are also limits to how much one person can do. Mother Teresa is pointed to as one who embodies the spirit of the Servant offering care to the most unfortunate. However, she does not directly confront the societal systems that produce such suffering. This task perhaps is for others who feel called to that work.

The role of the Suffering Servant is akin to that of the prophet. In *The Prophetic Imagination*, theologian Walter Brueggemann illuminates three aspects of the prophet's role in biblical times and today.[3] It is:

1. to grieve over, call attention to and/or identify with an existing situation of oppression or suffering; and then

2. to voice an alternative consciousness (that is, to articulate another way); and next,

3. to embody this alternative and thereby live the new way.

Twenty years ago, some people grieved over nine hundred children packed into a huge receiving home called Junior Village in the District of Columbia. Several studies had exposed shocking conditions.

A handful of individuals felt there had to be a better way. Starting out, they went door-to-door asking if neighbors would offer foster care to one Junior Village youngster. Soon this informal group formed FLOC (For Love of Children) and dug in for the long haul. Gradually they have evolved alternative structures that are humane and effective in helping disadvantaged children and families gain a surer footing: smaller group homes; an advocacy program to propose new legislation; a learning center to educate at-risk children; a Wilderness School for those who cannot succeed in city schools; the project Hope and a Home, which provides affordable housing to families; the project Manna, which trains inner-city dwellers in construction and rehabilitation skills.

FLOC people carry a triple stress: the suffering that occurs in the lives of the people they serve; the conflict involved in managing a complex organization composed of special-interest groups; and the challenge of working with structures and individuals in the larger municipal human-resources system. FLOC members create ways to enable honest sharing between affluent and poor. They form and re-form themselves as an alternative to existing institutions but in productive relationship with them. And they confront established institutions without alienating them, continuing the conversation even when they do not fully agree with them.

These are the tough challenges faced by FLOC members who share the spirit of the Suffering Servant. Their days are laced with moments when a family is reunited or a student returns to school. But there are low times when the mother of four uses the rent money to fill the cupboard with junk food or when FLOC people must face belittling attitudes of those who do not respect their work.

If the suffering has anything to say, it is that this kind of per-sistent, faithful, self-giving love even when things are hard makes real what Second Isaiah saw in a vision:

> Lo, I am about to create new heavens
> and a new earth;
> The things of the past shall not be remembered
> or come to mind.
> Instead, there shall always be rejoicing and happiness
> in what I create.
> (Isa. 65:17–18, NAB)

## GROUP DESIGN

*Purpose:* To reflect on the meaning of God as Suffering Servant for the Hebrew people and for us.

*Materials:* 8½ x 11 paper, marking pens, Bibles.

## A. Gathering Time, Large Group (*twenty minutes*)

Feel free to gather the group informally through sharing and prayer in whatever way is appropriate to your group. A suggestion is to share one thing that draws you to the group and its purpose of deeper growth and one thing that deflects you from it. Then gather these thoughts and feelings into a prayer of offering for each one and for the work of this session.

## B. Sharing Groups (*twenty minutes*)

Share briefly what you did with the suggestions for Individual Work after Session 4 and what this meant to you. Give each person a chance to speak before responding or entering into discussion. Remember, this profound subject does not lend itself to easy interpretation or application. The purpose of this time is to touch base with one another about what you did with the suggestions and not necessarily to resolve all the questions and issues involved, which are something to ponder over time.

## C. Suffering Servant Then, Large Group (*forty minutes*)

If necessary, someone should first summarize the session material on the Suffering Servant. Second, follow this procedure or one of your own devising to look at the poem and reflect on its meaning.

1.   Make sure everyone has a blank sheet of paper and some marking pens at hand. You can put your collection of markers in the center of the room, and people can choose what they need. Then everyone settle into silent receptivity.

2.   Each one open a Bible to Isa. 52:12–15—53:1–12. One person read the entire poem aloud slowly and reflectively.

3.   In the silence, each person reflect on these questions: According to the writer of this poem, when all is lost, how does love come through? What is the new dimension of love that is being lifted up? What new way of being is described?

4.   As you reflect, journal on your scrap paper with marking pens, portraying in lines, colors, words, or shapes what this poem tells you about God's love.

5.   When all are finished, place your papers on the floor in the middle of the group. Then whoever wishes may share what

you drew and why. You may have some light moments as each person tries to figure out what others drew, but also some important insights.

## D. Suffering Servant Now, Pairs and Large Groups (*thirty minutes*)

1. Take a few minutes of silence to think of someone you know or have heard about who exemplifies the spirit of the Suffering Servant. Has there been a time when God or a person reached out to you and you experienced in your own life the self-giving love that Isaiah was describing?

2. Choose someone with whom you have not as yet shared. Speak to each other about what occurred to you in your time of silent reflection.

3. Return to the large group and discuss the meaning of the Suffering Servant for you today.

## E. Closing, Large Group (*ten minutes*)

Choose one or two of the following suggestions as appropriate for your group: evaluation of session, song, details of next session, prayer of thanks for God's love as shown to us by Isaiah.

## INDIVIDUAL WORK

1. If you wish, read again the passage used in the session, Isa. 52:12–15—53:1–12.

2. Write in the first person as if you were God sending a message to you. Describe the love God has for you and for all people as portrayed in the Suffering Servant idea. In other words, write

yourself a message of God's love as you find it expressed through the Suffering Servant. Take off from the text, be freewheeling, make it personal. For example:

> Dear Bill:
>
> My love for you is like that of a person who gives everything for someone he loves. . . .

3. This week, in your periods of quiet, concentrate on receiving this aspect of God's love in a difficult area of your life. Bask in it.

4. *To prepare for next session:* Write a brief summary of your personal work with this assignment.

# SESSION 6

# A New Song

In the center of the collection of books we call the Bible are 150 prayers and songs called the Psalms. In four of these are the words,

> Sing to Yahweh
> a new song.[1]

These words invite us to call upon and notice God's presence today in whatever personal or social circumstances we find ourselves. The more we look for God, the more songs we sing. This session looks at how the Hebrew people sang to God and, in so doing, recognized God as new song. It then suggests how their songs can become ours and how those songs can stimulate us to compose our own.

When the Hebrew people looked at unfolding events, they often broke into song or poetry: sometimes praise for "the wonderful works of Yahweh" or pleas for deliverance from "the miry pit." Their songs not only let us in on intimate faith expressions from our spiritual ancestors, but also are a powerful prayer book for us today. Their words prayed by us mediate more dimensions of the divine than we might know by ourselves. Each psalm captures a fresh experience of God. These vivid expressions of honest feeling can inspire us to value and share our deepest selves in prayer.

This remarkable collection spans eight hundred years from the Exodus wanderings (ca. 1290 B.C.) to the Post-Exilic period (when the Temple was restored, 520 B.C.). Written by different authors, they reflect themes and ideas appropriate to the times in which they were composed. An angry god spouting fire and smoke, pictured in Psalm 17, represents early conceptions of Yahweh. Later a universal tone is heard in Psalm 117 (JB): "Praise Yahweh, all nations!"

In the Psalms, we find the range of human feelings that we all experience—sorrow, joy, gratitude, anger, pain, despair, praise. In his *Commentary on the Psalms*, John Calvin wrote:

> I may truly call this book an anatomy of all parts of the soul, for no one can feel a movement of the Spirit which is not reflected in this mirror.[2]

The English name is taken from the Greek word *psalmos*, meaning a song. Some of the songs, though not all, were used in temple worship, particularly for important feasts such as Passover (the commemoration of the deliverance), Pentecost, or the Feast of Weeks (the beginning of harvest), and Succoth, or Gathering-in (a week-long celebration like our Thanksgiving). The psalms were sung with musical instruments; rhythm was emphasized while melody was quite subordinate. The best known instrument was the harp, which resembled our lute or zither. The timbrel was like our tambourine. Cymbals, horns, trumpets, and reed pipes were also used.

An understanding of the different types of psalms enhances their meaning for us today. Mary Ellen Chase in *The Psalms for the Common Reader* offers a helpful classification: hymns for public worship, personal thanksgivings, personal and national lamentations, historical psalms to celebrate God's action in national events, psalms about nature, pilgrim songs for religious festivals, and psalms of personal meditation and reflection.[3]

The Psalms are still used by believers for both private and public worship. During the service, psalms are either read by the people or worship leader, or are sung in hymns and anthems.

Psalms have been prayed throughout the day by believers from earliest times; eventually compiled into the Liturgy of the Hours, this collection includes psalms for seven periods of the day, seven days a week. Some simplify this approach and pray psalms in the morning and evening as Matins and Evensong.

Perhaps most striking for the modern reader is the fact that the Psalms were the prayer book of Jesus. Twenty-one references to them are in the Gospel of Matthew. Study of these passages reveals that psalms were in Jesus' mind at important moments—at his baptism, in the desert temptations, as he was teaching, in the encounter with the money changers, in his confrontation over authority with the priests, and on the cross. It is clear that Jesus knew the Psalms well, meditating on them and using their words in prayer.

Dietrich Bonhoeffer, German pastor imprisoned by the Nazis during World War II, suggests that if we, like the disciples, want Jesus to teach us to pray, we would do well to pray with him the prayers he used, that is, to pray the Psalms.[4] There are many ways to do this. Some people use all or parts of the Liturgy of the Hours either regularly or whenever they can. In this way, they feel tied to the ongoing prayer of those who are committed to praying it daily. One of our class members, knowing that busy people might have a hard time with this, suggested that we use Psalm 95 as our opening morning prayer; it is the opening prayer of Matins, the first Hour of the Liturgy. This is a wonderful way to start the day:

> Come, let us praise Yahweh joyfully,
> acclaiming the Rock of our safety . . .
> (Ps. 95:1, JB)

Another way to pray the psalms is to find those that strike a chord in you. Then use selected phrases as a short repeated prayer. For example:

Look after me, God,
I take shelter in you.
(Ps. 16:1, JB)

You . . . give light to my lamp;
You brighten the darkness about me.
(Ps. 18:29, NAB)

Show me your way
And lead me on a level path.
(Ps. 27:11, NAB)

My heart is ready, O God,
My heart is ready!
(Ps. 108:1, RSV)

Although lists and classifications of the psalms are available, some people find it useful to do their own indexing so that they can readily find the psalms that are most helpful to them in times of joy or sorrow, for consolation, anchoring, or empowering. Some will have favorites for certain times of the day. In addition to Psalm 95, the first lines of Psalm 108 are a beautiful way to start the day. At nighttime, Psalms 63 and 131 are appropriate. Psalm 121 is particularly reassuring when contemplating the death of a loved one.

The psalms are enhanced for us when we know how other people use them. Do you remember the awesome moment when Neil Armstrong, first man on the moon, broadcast this psalm back to us?

When I look at your heavens, the work of your fingers,
the moon and the stars which you have established;
what are human beings that you are mindful of them,
and mortals that you care for them?

> Yet you have made them little less than a god,
> and crowned them with glory and honor.
> *(Ps. 8:3–5)*[5]

Fighting for the right of Soviet Jews to emigrate to Israel, Natan Sharansky was arrested by the KGB in Moscow. Soon after his imprisonment, his wife, Avital, gave him a Psalm Book. Robert Raines describes the result:

> Though not an actively religious person, he began to read the psalms in Hebrew, memorized entire psalms, and found astounding reassurance and comfort. . . . Their prayers became his own, taking him deep into his soul, preserving sanity and hope. . . . He knew he had to have that nourishment for the marrow of his soul, to strengthen his inner resistance and keep open the "interconnection of souls" which so encouraged him.[6]

Raines also describes his own experience with the Psalms:

> I was rummaging around in Psalm 119 one morning, delighting in the trove of nourishing phrases: "Let your steadfast love become my comfort . . . I treasure your word in my heart." I spoke those last words aloud, tasted them, heard them, felt them sink into my heart.

"Who can estimate the value of a few faith-filled words living in the heart?" asks Raines, and adds, "Words that bless, heal, illumine and encourage us become holy in our hearts."[7]

One way to appreciate God's presence more fully through the Psalms is to change the words so that you hear God speaking to you through them. For example, instead of praying, "The Lord is my shepherd," stop and hear God speaking to you:

> I am your shepherd.
> You will not want, because
> I will lead you beside
> still waters and
> restore your soul.
> (*Adapted from Ps. 23:1–3*)

In hard times when the Hebrew people needed assurance that God would deliver them, they would remember how that had happened in the past. They would pray, "You delivered our people from Egypt; please aid us now in trouble."

We can do the same thing, using a remembrance of God's earlier presence to strengthen us today. This is a good way to summarize your experience of God as you have worked through this book.

To do this, first remember that God creates out of chaos, calls us to companionship and collaboration, delivers us from bondage, invites us into a covenant relationship, enters into our suffering, and brings new life.

To compose your own song to God, describe your awareness of God and your response as you have pondered the Hebrew Scriptures. Or sound a note of praise, lament, pleading, questioning, or thanksgiving.

Here's a psalm written by a young person struggling with important decisions. It makes a fitting end to our exploration:

> Out of my chaos
> You spoke your name
> and took me through
> to a pact with you
> O Lord how you suffered
> Thanks, Lord, hear this song.[8]

# GROUP DESIGN

*Purpose:* To summarize the meaning of the course and to share next steps.

## A. Gathering Time, Large Group *(ten minutes)*

Gather the group informally through sharing and prayer. A suggestion would be to describe one time this week when God's love was apparent or one time when it seemed absent or hard to recognize. Then gather your thoughts and feelings into a prayer of offering for each one and for the work of this session.

## B. Sharing Groups *(twenty minutes)*

Go around the group and describe what you did with the individual work (feelings, learnings, difficulties). Then, if time permits, have some free discussion.

## C. Group Psalm Writing: A Way to Sing a New Song to God *(forty minutes)*

1. If necessary, one person summarize the material in the text about the Psalms. End with a quick review of the entire course material. (See the last four paragraphs in the text.)

2. Then, following the suggestion in the text, each one write your own new song to God relating to the material in the course. One way to do this is to compose a first line relating to what God did in history as Creator, then a companion line as your response today. Then write the next two lines on God as Caller in history and your response. Feel free to depart from this form and create your own. A way to begin might be to do a little free journaling on these questions:

✤ What newness has happened to you in the course?

✤ Does a next step suggest itself to you at this point?

3.   When all have finished writing, those who wish to may share their new songs in the large group. If you prefer, you might want to share in pairs and then have a few share in the large group. Remember that anyone is free not to share.

## D. Celebrating Newness and Sharing Next Steps, Large Group (*thirty minutes*)

1.   Take a few minutes of silence to look over your notes and finish any journaling you may have begun on newness and next steps.

2.   Spontaneously share your learnings, feelings, and ideas for next steps. Give everyone a chance to speak before opening up for general response and discussion. You might like to describe one place you want to move toward, one step to begin, and one obstacle that might stand in your way.

## E. Closing Celebration, Large Group (*ten minutes*)

In prayer and song or in any other ways your group might devise, express thanks to one another and to God for this time together.

## INDIVIDUAL WORK

(For people who are working with this course by themselves)

*Purpose:* To summarize your experience of this course, reflect on its overall meaning for you, and consider possible next steps.

Referring to section A in the Group Design, write in your journal a time this week when God's love was apparent and/or one time when it seemed absent or hard to recognize. If it seems right, let your journal writing lead you into a time of prayer. Because the previous session dealt with the theme of suffering, your prayer might focus on areas of suffering in your immediate environment or in the wider world that are of concern to you.

Refer to section C, Group Psalm Writing, in the Group Design.

1. Look back over the course material and any written work you have done.

2. Follow the suggestions at the end of the session text and in section C, number 2 of the Group Design. Write your own new song, or psalm, as a summary and prayer expressing your experience with the major themes of this course.

3. Consider speaking about your experience of this course with a friend or trusted person, possibly sharing any sense of newness or growth, questions, or disappointments.

4. Read the section entitled Next Steps.

# NEXT STEPS

When course participant Ricci Waters first heard about the Covenant, she had the feeling of coming home. She understood Covenant especially through Hosea, whose wife had run off. Hosea likened his experience to that of God who created us and lived the Covenant with us in love only to see us distance ourselves. The cry of God, as voiced by Hosea, was an invitation to come back home to live with God in love. Verses from a Weston Priory song paraphrase the poignant message of Hosea:

> Come back to me, with all your heart.
> Don't let fear keep us apart . . .
> Long have I waited for your coming home to me
> And living deeply our new life.[1]

Ricci Waters said, "It was easy for me to feel kicked out of my parents' house because when I left at seventeen, my father shouted, 'Don't ever come back again.' When I heard that Hosea's wife, Gomer, was invited back not because she followed the rules, but because Hosea loved her, I realized that God loves you not because of what you do but because of who you are.

"The Weston Priory song kicked up 'home' stuff for me. It opened up in me something that had been closed—you could trust God. It was an invitation to come home to stay. If you fell off the tightrope, it was there. The idea that drew me was the language of love, hearing God say, 'I love you, I want you to be with me.'

"This enabled me to take some first steps in trust. There was a shifting of sand under my feet. Whereas before I was fearful and closed, now I was open and trusting."

We hope that the exploration of Hebrew experiences of God contained in this book has opened you, like Ricci, to discover their power for you. After taking time to absorb what you have learned, you might like to continue with another book in the *Doorways* Series.

A natural sequel is to look at Jesus afresh, to see how his life and work flowed from Hebrew discoveries about God. This you can do through *Meeting Jesus in the New Testament*. You will then have an overview of biblical understandings of the divine and how they can empower your life.

If you would like more specific suggestions for living the Covenant through the vital spiritual practices used by believers to deepen their experience of God, consider *Journeying with the Spirit*.

For more details on your calling to collaborate in God's dream for all people, see *Discovering Your Gifts, Vision, and Call*. This links calling with God's vision and the particular gifts you have been given.

Dorothy Day was one who lived the life of faith with extraordinary commitment. Remarks on the jacket of the book of her selected writings summarize her life work:

> A co-founder in 1933 (with the French peasant philosopher Peter Maurin) of the Catholic Worker movement, and for almost fifty years editor and publisher of its newspaper, she applied the Gospels to a sweeping radical critique of our economic, social, and political systems and addressed the most urgent issues of our time: poverty, labor, justice, civil liberties, and disarmament. She saw the movement as an affirmation of life and sanity, and a way to "bring about the kind of society where it is easier to be good."[2]

What was striking about Dorothy Day, according to the editor of her writings, "was not what she wrote . . . nor what she believed, but the fact that there was absolutely no distinction between what she believed, what she wrote, and the manner in which she lived."[3]

How did the life of faith begin for Dorothy Day? An important influence was her childhood friend, Mary Harrington, a twelve-year-old with whom she often talked and dreamed. One evening Mary told Dorothy the life of some saint. Dorothy later wrote this about the incident:

> I don't remember which one, nor can I remember any of the incidents of it. I can only remember the feeling of lofty enthusiasm I had, how my heart seemed only bursting with desire to take part in such high endeavor. One verse of the Psalms often comes to my mind: "Enlarge Thou my heart, O Lord, that Thou mayest enter in." This was one of those occasions when my small heart was enlarged.[4]

This is the hope we have for the books in the *Doorways* Series: that they may create opportunities for our hearts to be enlarged that we may welcome God's love more deeply and share it more fully.

# ADDITIONAL RESOURCES

Two studies of creativity mentioned in the notes have been valuable companions in our endeavor to understand what it means to be a co-creator with God:

May, Rollo. *The Courage to Create*. New York: W. W. Norton, 1975.

Robbins, Lois. *Waking Up in the Age of Creativity*. Santa Fe: Bear and Company, 1985.

For more on the importance of story and image, see:

Campbell, Joseph, with Bill Moyers. *The Power of Myth*. New York: Doubleday, 1991.

Houston, Jean. *The Search for the Beloved*. Los Angeles: J. P. Tarcher, 1987.

Creation spirituality builds on the theme of creation and co-creation. Major work is being done in this by Matthew Fox. The following books would be a place to learn more:

Fox, Matthew. *Original Blessing*. Santa Fe: Bear and Company, 1983.

Fox, Matthew. *Creation Spirituality: Liberating Gifts for the Peoples of the Earth*. San Francisco: HarperSanFrancisco, 1991.

For fuller background and understanding of the God in Hebrew Scripture, these books are helpful:

Brueggemann, Walter. *The Prophetic Imagination*. Philadelphia: Fortress Press, 1978.

Brueggemann, Walter. *Praying the Psalms*. Winona, MN: St. Mary's Press, 1982.

Women are bringing fresh perspective to the interpretation of biblical stories and images:

Bankson, Marjory Zoet. *Braided Streams: Esther and a Woman's Way of Growing*. San Diego: LuraMedia, 1985.

Trible, Phyllis. *Texts of Terror: Literary-Feminist Readings of Biblical Narratives*. Philadelphia: Fortress Press, 1984.

Weems, Renita J. *Just a Sister Away*. San Diego: LuraMedia, 1988.

For more on how to evolve a spiritual practice that is right for you:

Anderson, Sherry Ruth, and Hopkins, Patricia. *The Feminine Face of God*. New York: Bantam Books, 1991.

May, Gerald G. *The Awakened Heart: Living Beyond Addiction*. San Francisco: HarperSanFrancisco, 1991.

Environmental theology explores creation themes. For related readings see:

Andrews, Valerie, *A Passion for the Earth: Exploring a New Partnership of Man, Woman and Nature*. San Francisco: HarperSanFrancisco, 1990.

Berry, Thomas. *The Dream of the Earth*. San Francisco: Sierra Club, 1988.

Native American spirituality offers a perspective deeply respectful of the Earth. For a compilation of Native American writings, see:

McLuhan, T. C. *Touch the Earth: A Self-Portrait of Indian Existence*. New York: Simon and Schuster, 1971.

To continue the growth process offered in the *Doorways* Series, consider:

*Meeting Jesus in the New Testament*. To understand how Jesus related to God and to see how he can ground us more deeply in God's love and justice.

*Journeying with the Spirit.* To experience time-honored tools
for growth such as prayer, meditation, healing, reconciliation, exploring God's presence over the span of our lives.
*Discovering Your Gifts, Vision, and Call.* To continue exploration of call and to relate that with God's vision and
our gifts.

The *Doorways* Series, when offered in a parish, can be a catalyst for change in individuals and in the congregation. To learn
more about how a parish can foster the spiritual journeys of members plus organize to support each one's vision, call, and gifts, in-
quire about the authors' "Recreating the Church" packet of
articles: 1309 Merchant Lane, McLean, VA 22101.

As a follow-up to this course, some people have found value
in reading the Scriptures selected for the coming Sunday liturgy.
Typically these include a selection from the Hebrew Scriptures,
the Psalms, the Epistles, and the Gospels. Many churches follow
an ecumenical lectionary shared by Roman Catholic and a number of Protestant denominations. By meditating on these readings,
one joins the rhythm of the liturgical year and the many churches
around the world using them.

# ACKNOWLEDGMENTS

Like all books, this one has a story behind it. Telling that story allows us to thank all the people who helped along the way and also gives you, the reader, some background on how this was written and why.

In a sense this book began when Lois Donnelly, a Catholic, joined with Jackie McMakin and Pat Davis, both Protestants, to offer workshops and courses in local churches. Jean Sweeney and Rhoda Nary, both Catholics, soon joined us. We took the name Partners because we experienced great creativity when as Catholics and Protestants we partnered together to do our work.

Some of us received training in experiential design from Faith at Work. We were inspired by the work of the Taizé Community in France, started by Roger Schutz, a Swiss Reformed pastor, who drew together Roman Catholic and Protestant men to live a monastic life dedicated to "a passion for unity."

Becoming dissatisfied with our "piecemeal" workshops and courses, we were ready for what became a life-changing question: "If you could do anything you wanted in churches, what would it be?"

We had been students at the Church of the Saviour's School of Christian Living and had been deeply affected by the courses offered there. Founded by Gordon and Mary Cosby, its story has been chronicled by Elizabeth O'Connor. Could we design a similar set of courses that would present the treasures of both Catholic and Protestant traditions in a format that busy people could respond to?

What resulted were the four courses contained in the *Doorways* Series. When they were offered, several participants wanted to join us in the Partners Community: Susan Hogan, Cathie

Bates, Dave Scheele, Mid Allen, Ricci Waters, Sally Dowling, Sancy Scheele, Coby Pieterman, and Charlotte Rogers. Each of these people added their ideas to the courses as we developed them further.

Participants then began to ask, "Could you give us the course materials so we could facilitate them ourselves and take them to other places?"

Jackie began to translate the notes and outlines into book form but soon got bogged down. Rhoda volunteered to help, and from then on we worked together, Jackie as writer, Rhoda as editor, both as conceptualizers. The Partners gave tremendous support throughout the process and helped a great deal with finishing touches. Others who helped were Mim Dinndorf, Sonya Dyer, Mary Elizabeth Hunt, Maggie Kalil, Gertrude Kramer, Billie Johansen, Mary Pockman, Janet Rife, Mary Scantlebury, and Gretchen Hannon. Our first editor was Cy Riley from Winston Press.

Liberation, black, creation, and feminist theologies have shown us how limited are our contemporary thought patterns and organizational structures. These theologies stress the Gospel's "preferential option for the poor," the importance of valuing and incorporating the experience of nonwhite, Third World, female, oppressed, and marginalized persons.

In such a theologically fertile period, when new understandings are being lived, shared, and written about at an amazing rate, each choice of word, phrase, or emphasis has theological implications. Whatever we write, in one sense, is quickly dated. Yet, in another sense, we are trying to capture and describe some of the timeless aspects of Christian faith. This book would serve a good purpose if our attempts to preserve the old and incorporate the new stimulated each of you to do this personally.

Since first published in 1984, the *Doorways* Series has found its way to several countries outside our own, most notably Mexico.

There it has enjoyed wide use. A Spanish translation called *Puertas al Encuentro*, including Mexican examples, was created by Mari Carmen Mariscal and associates.[1] Several stories of our Mexican friends are included in this revision.

For this new edition, we are indebted to editor Kandace Hawkinson for seeing the possibility of a brand-new format—each course presented in a single book. She and her fellow editor, Ron Klug, have been wonderful to work with. Others here at home have been a big help, some for the second time: Millie Adams, Marjorie Bankson, Connie Francis, Lynn Pareut, Ellen Radday, Gay Bland, Gretchen Hannon, Martha Hlavin, Mary Moore, and Valerie Vesser. Our husbands, Dave McMakin and Bill Nary, and our children, Tom and Peg McMakin and Brendan, Kristin, Kevin, and Paul Nary, have given lots of support, each in different ways.

We would like to hear from you about any reactions and suggestions you have that will help improve this approach to strengthening your spiritual life. If you would like us to partner with you as you consider next steps after using the *Doorways* Series, we are available for consultation, training, and retreats.

Jacqueline McMakin
1309 Merchant Lane
McLean, VA 22101
(703) 827–0336

Rhoda Nary
4870 N 27th Place
Arlington, VA 22207
(703) 538–6132

# NOTES

*Introduction*

1. Christopher Bryant, *Jung and the Christian Way* (Minneapolis: Seabury Press, 1983), p. 1.

2. Joseph Campbell with Bill Moyers, *The Power of Myth* (New York: Doubleday, 1991), p. 4.

3. Virginia Mollenkott, *The Divine Feminine* (New York: Crossroad Publishing, 1983).

4. Verna J. Dozier, *The Dream of God* (Boston: Cowley Publications, 1991), p. 30.

5. Dozier, *Dream of God*, p. 20.

6. Dozier, *Dream of God*, p. 60.

*Session 1*

1. Sadly, two phrases in the story have been used to sanction humankind's domination over the Earth. In some translations, Gen. 1:26 speaks of people as "subduing" or "ruling" the Earth and its creatures. The Hebrew words used there suggest "serving" or "caring for" rather than domination.

   Some contemporary writers draw on Native American sources to encourage respect for the Earth. Thomas Berry in *The Dream of the Earth* (San Francisco: Sierra Club Books, 1990) and Valerie Andrews in *A Passion for This Earth* (San Francisco: HarperSanFrancisco, 1990), for example, put forward the idea of the Earth as our generous teacher and humankind as learner of its wisdom.

2. Verna J. Dozier, *The Dream of God* (Boston: Cowley Publications, 1991), pp. 28, 29.

3. Matthew Fox, *Original Blessing* (Santa Fe: Bear and Company, 1983), p. 231.

4. Rollo May, *The Courage to Create* (New York: Bantam Books, 1978).

5. May, *The Courage to Create*, p. 37.

6. May, *The Courage to Create*, p. 15.

7. May, *The Courage to Create*, pp. 1–2.

8. May, *The Courage to Create*, p. 64.

9. May, *The Courage to Create*, p. 3.

10. Robert McAfee Brown, *The Bible Speaks to You* (Philadelphia: Westminster Press, 1960), p. 39.

11. Brown, *The Bible Speaks*, p. 41.

*Session 2*

1. Dag Hammarskjöld, *Markings* (New York: Alfred A. Knopf, 1964), p. 205.

2. "A Personal Pilgrimage: Experiences of Common Contemplatives," in *The Wind Is Rising*, William R. Callahan, S.J., and Francine Cardman, eds. (Hyattsville, MD: Quixote Center, 1978), p. 27.

3. Morris West, *The Clowns of God* (New York: Bantam Books, 1981), pp. 118–19.

4. Anne Keith, essay in *Profiles in Ministry* (sketches of thirteen ministering people), published by Working from the Heart, 1309 Merchant Lane, McLean, VA 22101 in 1985.

## Session 3

1. *The Washington Post*, January 8, 1992, pp. 1 and 17.

2. *The Washington Post*.

3. *Time*, December 16, 1991, p. 20.

4. *The Washington Post*.

5. Inclusive Language Lectionary Committee, *An Inclusive Language Lectionary, Readings for Year C*, p. 209.

6. An address to the First Annual Community Forum on Breast Cancer, Los Angeles, May 3, 1980. Reprinted with permission.

7. Rose Elizabeth Bird, address, May 3, 1980.

8. Karl A. Olsson, *Find Yourself in the Bible* (Minneapolis: Augsburg Publishing, 1974), pp. 37–43.

9. Harold S. Kushner, *When Bad Things Happen to Good People* (New York: Avon Books, 1983), p. 141.

10. Kushner, *When Bad Things Happen*, p. 136.

11. Kushner, *When Bad Things Happen*, p. 142.

12. Kushner, *When Bad Things Happen*, p. 139.

## Session 4

1. Inclusive Language Lectionary Committee, *An Inclusive Language Lectionary* (Philadelphia: Westminster Press, 1983), Epiphany 8.

2. Mary Clare Powell, *The Widow* (Washington, DC: Anaconda Press, 1981), pp. 58–59. (Limited supply of books available from Ruth Powell, 49F Ridge Road, Greenbelt, MD 20770.)

3. Patricia M. Mische, "Earth Covenant: The Evolution of a Citizen's Treaty for Common Ecological Security." This article and the Earth Covenant are distributed by Global Education Associates, 475 Riverside Drive, Suite 456, New York, NY 10115.

## Session 5

1. The Book of Isaiah is thought to be the work of at least three writers. Chapters 40–55 are the work of an unknown writer sometimes called Isaiah of Babylon, or Second Isaiah.

2. Inclusive Language Lectionary Committee, *An Inclusive Language Lectionary, Readings for Year B*, p. 208.

3. Walker Brueggemann, *The Prophetic Imagination* (Philadelphia: Fortress, 1978).

## Session 6

1. Psalms 96, 98, and 149.

2. Quoted by Mary Ellen Chase in *Psalms for the Common Reader* (New York: W. W. Norton, 1962), p. 25.

3. Quoted by Chase in *Psalms*, pp. 37–69 and 121–59.

4. Mary Ellen Chase, *Psalms: The Prayer Book of the Bible* (Minneapolis: Augsburg Publishing, 1970), pp. 13–16.

5. Inclusive Language Lectionary Committee, *An Inclusive Language Lectionary, Readings for Year C*, p. 158.

6. This is a paraphrase of Robert Raines's article on Sharansky. The quotations are Raines's words. Printed in *The Ridgeleaf*, no. 169 (September 1988).

7. Raines, *The Ridgeleaf*, no. 188 (January 1992).

8. Written by Vicki Garneau. Used with permission.

*Next Steps*

1. *Listen*, Weston Priory Productions, Weston, Vermont, 1972.

2. Dorothy Day, *By Little and By Little: The Selected Writings of Dorothy Day*, Robert Ellsberg, ed. (New York: Alfred A. Knopf, 1983), jacket.

3. Day, *By Little*, jacket.

4. Day, *By Little*, p. 12.

*Acknowledgments*

1. Available from Edamex, Heriberto Frias #1104, Mexico 03100, D. F. Mexico, or from the authors.